The Hypnosis I Know

DAWN WHEELER

The Hypnosis I Know
Copyright © 2014   Dawn Wheeler
ISBN: 1495377725
ISBN-13: 978-1495377723

All Rights Reserved. No part of this book may be reproduced or transmitted in any form or by any means, electronic or mechanical, including photocopying, recording or by any information storage and retrieval system, without written permission from the author, except for the inclusion of brief quotations in a review.

The techniques presented in this book should not be attempted by anyone other than a professional hypnotherapist. The information contained within this book is not intended to be used for diagnosis or treatment of any issue, physical, emotional, mental or otherwise. Readers should consult with a physician or qualified health professional in matters related to their well-being, particularly with respect to any symptoms that may require diagnosis or medical attention or treatment. The author assumes no responsibility for any individual's interpretation or use of this information.

On A Clear Day (You Can See Forever)
Words by Alan Jay Lerner
Music by Burton Lane
Copyright © 1965 (Renewed) Chappell & Co., Inc.
All Rights Reserved.

DEDICATION

This book is dedicated to the memory of my mother Phyllis who opened my eyes to the magic and mystery of the universe very early on and helped shape who I am today. I love and miss you Mommy.

CONTENTS

Acknowledgments   vii

Introduction   1

Chapter 1: Hypnosis - The Misunderstood Child   15

Chapter 2: What's In A Mind   20

Chapter 3: Creating Beliefs, Perceptions & Behavior Patterns   35

Chapter 4: Goal-Driven Border Guard - Ready For Duty   42

Chapter 5: Feelings, So Much More Than Feelings   51

Chapter 6: Blockages, Buttons & Triggers - Oh My!   61

Chapter 7: It's A Habit   69

Chapter 8: Other Oddities We Store   75

Chapter 9: What Is Hypnosis?   81

Chapter 10: Hypnosis Is Natural   93

Chapter 11: A Good Hypnotherapist   100

Chapter 12:	Just Ask	107
Chapter 13:	Hypnotic Techniques & Perspectives	111
Chapter 14:	The Regression Controversy	118
Chapter 15:	Other Hypnotic Techniques & Perspectives	134
Chapter 16:	It's A Miracle	146
Chapter 17:	That's Karma For You	155
Chapter 18:	Energy Affects Energy	167
Chapter 19:	The Entity Factor	174
Chapter 20:	Other Spiritual Phenomenon	189
Chapter 21:	It's A Process	196
Conclusion		202

ACKNOWLEDGMENTS

To the many people who encouraged me to write this book - Thank you for your belief in me and the work I do. I hope this book meets with your approval.

To my teachers - Thank you for sharing your wisdom and experience.

To my clients - Thank you for letting me be part of your journey and for the opportunity to witness the amazing resilience of the human spirit and body. Your stories and transformations have truly inspired and humbled me.

To my awesome hypno-buddies Marie and Pat - It's been a wild ride thus far. Here's to more adventures!

To my book reviewers and proofreaders extraordinaire: Philip, Marie, Kyle, Caroline & Kathy - Thank you for your time, feedback and support.

And last but certainly not least, to my wonderful husband Philip - Thank you for your love, support, wisdom and humor and being who you are. I love you.

Life can sometimes feel like being trapped in the midst of a chaotic storm, swirling with darkness and debris, and no perceivable way out. But there is a way out. Seeking out the stillness of one's mind, challenging limiting perceptions and unloading the burdens of the past can allow a person to break free from the darkness and find a path to peace, joy and light. No one has to stay in the storm. Anyone can leave, if they choose. Hypnosis can help a person uncover the way to freedom. Once the path is revealed, all one needs to do is take it. And when they do, everything will seem possible.

INTRODUCTION

Who am I? Am I the name I was given upon my birth? It is true, people often refer to us by our name, and names do have a certain energy and symbolism of their own, but is it really who we are? William Shakespeare confronts the often deceiving aspect of relying too heavily on names to describe something or someone when he says, "What's in a name? That which we call a rose by any other name would smell as sweet." He's right of course. So, if we are not our names, perhaps it is what we do that says who we are. Many people define themselves by the jobs they hold, the roles they play or the purpose they fulfill or fail to fulfill in their daily lives. Teacher, lawyer, doctor, secretary, engineer, programmer, salesperson, chef or housekeeper.

Mother, father, daughter, son, husband, wife, boyfriend or girlfriend. These jobs and roles do say a lot about us, but again, are they really who we are?

Humanity loves to quantify aspects of life in order to define people and measure their value. How much money do they make? Do they rent or own? Are they married? Do they have children? Do they own a computer, cell phone or flat screen TV? Do they purchase their clothes from upper-end retailers or do they buy them from discount stores or even thrift shops? Does any of this really matter? Are we really only a compilation of superficial elements subject to public opinion? Do we have value if we have nothing or no one in our life?

I believe that it is our choices that define us rather than our more external aspects. I also believe that everyone has value no matter what. I view human beings as multi-dimensional manifestations of body, mind, spirit and energy and recognize that it's up to each individual to travel their own personal journey through life in order to find the answers they are seeking. And when we are ready, we will know who we really are.

I have always been curious in nature and enjoy learning new things. I am especially fascinated by that which is deemed beyond explanation or topics which many people disagree about. As long as I can remember, I viewed the world through an idealist's eyes and saw beyond the limits that many perceived. I also believed that something could exist even though we may lack a means to prove it and had faith in things that others only hoped were real.

To disregard that which is unseen, unproven or controversial is unwise. To avoid even discussing the possibilities that exist in this world is just tragic. Unfortunately, it's done all the time. A wonderful quote from the musical movie "1776" captures this concept brilliantly. When the vote was tied regarding the question of whether or not to debate the feasibility of American independence, it was all up to one person to determine whether or not it would pass. Before casting his vote, Rhode Island representative Stephen Hopkins made the following statement, "Well, in all my years I ain't never heard, seen, nor smelled an issue that was so dangerous it couldn't be talked about. Hell yeah! I'm for debating anything. Rhode Island says yea!"

I cannot even imagine what the world would be like today if the Continental Congress failed to debate, let alone declare independence from Britain. The United States of America and all that it does and represents in the world would not exist, if not for the few and brave who were willing to risk everything including their lives to travel down unchartered waters in hopes of creating something new and better.

Beyond the political trailblazers of our nation's history, there are many more people today thinking outside the box, asking questions and exploring the unknown in hopes of making the world a better place and giving its inhabitants a higher quality of life. Unfortunately, breaking through the deeply rooted fears of humanity and awakening both curiosity and receptivity to change can be a daunting task. Consider for example, that it took more than three centuries for the Catholic Church to admit any wrongdoing for condemning the astronomer Galileo for heresy in suggesting that the earth revolves around the sun. Tragically, Galileo was forced to retract his scientific findings to avoid torture or death, and spent the remaining years of his life under house arrest. A brilliant man with a quest for knowledge and understanding was punished because he dared to challenge traditional thinking and teachings.

The power of the human mind and its potential for healing and transformation is unlimited, yet few on this planet have explored its possibilities. Much like with other perspectives which defy explanation or challenge existing ways of life, many people find even discussing body-mind related concepts to be uncomfortable or even taboo.

Thankfully, no topic was off limits for discussion in my own home while growing up. My mother, a seeker of knowledge in her own right, was open-minded and unafraid of talking about things that typically made people uncomfortable. Over the years, we conversed and philosophized about many controversial subjects including: religion, ghosts, reincarnation and UFO phenomenon.

INTRODUCTION

Although I didn't know it at the time, she was preparing me for the work I do now.

Aside from allowing my inquisitive nature to flourish, my mother always encouraged me to freely express my thoughts, ideas and feelings. I'm sure that many of the people in my past would have preferred that I was more introspective and less talkative, and even more so, less emotional. But whatch-ya gonna do. I am who I am. Unsurprisingly, emotional expression was destined to be a significant theme in my life.

Since I was a young child, I've been sensitive to the physical and emotional pain of others, and could at times feel what another person was feeling, even though I didn't always recognize it. As a result of my strong empathy for those around me, I became an advocate of sorts, frequently standing up for people who could not stand up for themselves. Many times in my early school years, I would feel compelled to confront a bully or a name-caller to try and make them stop being so hurtful. I remember coming home on multiple occasions crying to my mother about how terrible the world was. I simply could not understand why people were so cruel, and found it difficult to understand why people put up with it.

Being sensitive not only made me the defender of the weak, it also made me an unofficial advisor, therapist, confession taker and pep-talk giver for anyone in my midst. It felt like I had a post-it note stuck to my forehead that said, "I care, so tell me about it." Friends, acquaintances and strangers alike gravitated to me with their problems, looking for some insight and comfort. It wasn't always easy, but I did my best.

I remember as far back as kindergarten listening to the troubles of five year olds in the play yard at recess. While working at a bank during college, customers frequently came to my window for a bit of advice and comfort along with their transaction. And while working in corporate America, I spent many breaks sitting in conference rooms listening to my co-worker's problems. And then there were the countless strangers throughout the years coming up to me on the street, in grocery stores, in restaurants and the like, sharing with me their stories and pain.

I suspect that others sought me out because they perceived me to be safe. Perhaps they were also drawn to me because of my ability to see things in other people's situations that I couldn't see in my own life. Whether it was offering someone a different perspective, or helping one recognize the alternatives they had, or just listening and showing them that someone cared, I did what I could. Apparently it helped. I even used to joke with some of my closer friends how one day I would be doing this for a living. Who knew?

Despite the therapeutic sideline I had going, I have always been a practical sort. I went to college to study business and computer science. After graduation, I, like so

INTRODUCTION

many others before me, joined the ranks of corporate America to make a difference. I had many diverse and wonderful experiences during my career in the computer/business world. I was also very good at what I did and enjoyed a good deal of success as a result. But I had a problem.

I had values and I cared too much. I believed in honesty and fairness. I believed that you should always do your best and that if you do something, you should strive to do it right the first time. I also believed that it wasn't enough to point out problems or areas needing improvement, but to be part of the solution. I believed things that some of my management and fellow peers did not. My ethics, idealist view of the world, sense of personal responsibility and ability to anticipate issues made some people feel threatened. They thought I had some hidden desire to take over the place. I didn't want to take over. I just wanted to do a good job and I wanted the people around me to do a good job.

Eventually, I became weary of the toxic world of corporate and decided to leave. It was a hard decision, but looking back it was meant to be. Before I talk about how I began my work with hypnosis, I need to go further back in time.

I lost my mother 24 years ago. It was her heart, the same heart that loved me unconditionally and encouraged me to be who I was. She had the kind of heart that made her care about people and the world around her, and passionately fight for the principles in which she believed. Aside from being my mother, she was also my friend, advisor, and one of the few people I could come crying to. But suddenly she was gone.

Although part of me knew that my mother and I were not truly disconnected, I was devastated by her loss. The world carried on even though she was gone and so would I, but I would not be the same. I functioned as before, doing all the things I needed or was expected to do, and did them well. But something was missing. Many people feel that when someone they love dies, it's as if a piece of them is taken away, and they are left with a void that remains with them until they die. My mom's passing did leave a void in my life and heart. A few years after her death, I felt compelled to embark on a spiritual quest of sorts in an attempt to fill that void. While I will always miss my mother, I eventually achieved a sense of peace and wholeness.

Not long before my mother unexpectedly died, we were both reading "Many Lives Many Masters" by Dr. Brian Weiss. It's an inspiring and well written story based on a true case history. Dr. Weiss, a well respected classically trained psychiatrist, reluctantly finds his belief systems challenged when he decides to hypnotize a client who is not responding to traditional therapy. When he asks an open ended question intended to direct his client back to

INTRODUCTION

the source of her problem, it unexpectedly leads them both to another time and place, and propels them on a journey of healing and spiritual awareness.

Dr. Weiss put his reputation on the line to publish his highly controversial and life changing book. Thankfully, it paid off not only for himself but for the many lives it has touched over the years. My mother and I discussed this book at length and were excited that someone with Weiss' background and credentials was talking about life and death in such an expanded and wonderful way. Past lives, reincarnation, karma, whatever you want to call it, wasn't something people in Yale medical school typically discussed, but now one of their graduates was creating dialogues about this very concept in a very public way.

Just a few months after reading Weiss' book, for some unexplainable reason, I felt almost panicked about the potential of losing my mother. I told her she could not leave, because I would not be able to go on without her. She told me that no one can know when it is their time to go, but when her time comes, she said I must go on without her, and no matter how hard it may be, I would eventually be okay. I wasn't convinced, but decided not to bring it up again. My mother died about a year later. Coincidentally, her death occurred in the very hospital where Dr. Weiss had his practice.

I didn't know it then, but there would be another synchronicity later on that I would associate with Brian

Weiss, one that brings us back to my mission. Early on in my quest, I made the acquaintance of someone who worked in the same office, but whom I had not had the opportunity to work with before. One day, on the way to a meeting, I happened to be in the vicinity of her cubicle and noticed a flyer on her desk mentioning Dr. Weiss. I stopped to ask her about it. She was surprised to hear that I was well acquainted with Weiss let alone a wide variety of other metaphysically oriented things. Let's just say the corporate world wasn't a major new age hangout. Anyway, she told me he was giving a workshop locally that covered his own journey as well as information in his second book "Through Time into Healing" and then hesitantly asked if I was interested in going. I said yes.

That workshop began a wonderful friendship and a metaphysical journey to reclaim what I already knew and discover what more there was to know. It also became a path for my own healing and an awakening to who I really was and who I was meant to be. I met so many inspirational people in those years and had such life changing moments, I will forever be grateful.

When I decided to leave corporate, I was determined to keep my options open and take a totally different direction with my career. One path seemed to call to me more than others. I've always been fascinated by human behavior and motivation, as well as emotional pain. And of course, I've always enjoyed helping people. I also had a strong interest

INTRODUCTION

in the power of the mind. But because I've never really resonated with traditional psychology, I ruled out going back to school to become a psychologist. And although I dabbled with hypnosis in the past and found it to be intriguing, I hadn't truly considered doing it as a profession. There were many signs coaxing me toward hypnosis. I eventually followed them and enrolled in a state licensed hypnosis school.

As I read through the material and experimented with the state of hypnosis, I felt like I had come home. It was like emerging from a temporary state of amnesia. Suddenly, everything was so clear and even strangely familiar. I understood the often complex concepts that were being discussed and demonstrated, but more importantly, I saw the possibilities beyond them. And I got excited. Upon graduation and certification, I opened up my hypnotherapy practice to begin another amazing journey.

I call my company Mind Over Matter, a name I came up with early on in school. I felt it best captured what hypnosis was about. When I opened my office, it was bittersweet. I was happy about what I was setting out to do, but I felt sad that my mom could not be there to share it with me. My third client helped me discover that my mother was with me in this endeavor all along. They told me that the name of my business really spoke to them and was the main reason they decided to call. This client also mentioned that they really liked the acronym for my business and found it comforting. M.O.M, mom. I honestly never noticed it before, but there it was plain as day. My mother will always be part of what I do, and I will always be grateful for having her, even though our time together was brief.

It has been 16 years now, and the potential for hypnosis and the mind still excites me. The transformations I've witnessed and facilitated over the years have been truly awe inspiring. I sometimes wish I could travel back in time and hypnotize my mother, so that maybe she wouldn't have died so young. But I know that however sad it may be, she was meant to leave and I was meant to go on. I was meant to use her loss to fulfill my purpose on this earth. While I could not save my own mother, I've been able to help spare many others the premature loss of their mothers, fathers, spouses, siblings, friends and more over the years. And for that, I am very happy.

This book gives me an opportunity to share with you some of what I've learned and experienced in my work with hypnosis. I have written it in hopes that it will create new dialogues, expand the awareness of the power of the mind and the unseen aspects of the world, and inspire others along their journey for self-discovery and healing. I hope that one day, many people will come to know the hypnosis I know and let it change their lives for the better.

INTRODUCTION

When I first watched the movie "On a Clear Day" starring Barbara Streisand many years ago, I found myself highly intrigued by its depiction of hypnosis and its use in uncovering past lives. I let myself imagine for a brief moment what it would be like to hypnotize someone else, even though I never really thought I would ever do it. Despite its inaccuracies and tendency to propagate some of the typical misconceptions of hypnosis in almost ludicrous ways, the film is fun to watch and holds many truths within it. Perhaps the most important message one can take away from this zany musical comedy is that human beings are complex, mysterious and miraculous creatures who are all connected, even if they are unwilling to accept it. I believe that the tool of hypnosis offers a unique opportunity to create the clear day that Alan Jay Lerner's lyrics speak of in this movie's theme song.

You're a bloody miracle...
Could anyone among us have an inkling or a clue
What magic feats or wizardry and voodoo you can do?
And who would ever guess what powers you possess
And who would not be stunned to see you prove
There's more to us than surgeons can remove
So much more than we ever knew
So much more were we born to do
Should you draw back the curtain, this I am certain

THE HYPNOSIS I KNOW

You'll be impressed with you
On a clear day
Rise and look around you
And you'll see who you are
On a clear day
How it will astound you
That the glow of your being
Outshines every star
You'll feel part of every mountain, sea and shore
You can hear
From far and near
A world you've never, never heard before...
And on a clear day...On a clear day...
You can see forever...
And ever...
And ever...
And ever more

CHAPTER 1

HYPNOSIS - THE MISUNDERSTOOD CHILD

Hypnosis is like a poor misunderstood child. People frequently speak negatively about it and expect the worst of it, even though they haven't taken the time to get to know it. The mere mention of the word hypnosis seems to breed the most extreme responses amongst people, and more often than not, it is one of fear. I cannot tell you how many times someone has asked me not to look into their eyes when they discover I use hypnosis in my work. They are genuinely afraid that I will make them do something they have no desire to do. If I had that power, no one would ever disappoint me and best of all, this world would be a very different place. Trust me when I say, everyone can breathe easy, it's safe to look into my eyes.

Worse than thinking that someone can impose their will upon another by just looking into their eyes, there are many people who view hypnosis as witchcraft or the work of the devil. They believe that if a person was not evil before doing hypnosis, they will surely be after. These are probably the same people who thought the Harry Potter series should be banned. Why is it that when something makes people feel good and personally responsible for their own choices and life, and ultimately empowers and heals them, it is looked upon as bad or un-God-like? And why are the people who selflessly give of themselves to uplift, comfort, enlighten and empower others considered to be whack jobs, witches or crazed devil worshipers? In an attempt to ensure that they only experience good, small minded people fed by fear or the need to control others will never truly see the positive or the good. They will only see the opportunity to minimize others or reconfirm their own need to stay fearful. And most of all, they will miss out on the true God-like magic of the universe. How sad.

Aside from the usual concern over mind control or morality, most people associate hypnosis with dangling pocket watches, clucking like a chicken and stopping smoking.

It's troubling to me how little people know about hypnosis and the workings of their own minds, and more significantly, how little they want to know about it. Hypnosis has been around for many centuries, yet most people are unfamiliar with what it is and how it can be used to better their lives. The medical and psychiatric communities have recognized hypnosis as a viable therapeutic tool since the late 1950s, yet they place very little emphasis on its use. Also, most insurance plans exclude hypnosis from their coverage, despite the many cases which demonstrate its positive effect on the body and emotional well-being.

The field of medicine has revolutionized the way we live and made considerable headway over the years in extending life expectancy. Despite the important role it plays in the modern world, the solutions that traditional medicine offers are not always in line with what the public needs or wants. Desiring more effective and lasting results with less drastic measures and side effects, people are seeking more natural options. The pills that pharmaceutical companies push more heavily every day are starting to lose their allure. Complementary or alternative healing methodologies and treatments are growing in popularity and beginning to creep into mainstream healthcare. Unfortunately, this trend is progressing much too slowly. And sadly, hypnosis is getting a lot less attention than the others, even though it perhaps has greater potential.

Thanks to people like Dr. Weiss, the field of hypnosis has received some positive consideration. Along with his own, there are numerous books available on the subject. But even these many published works don't tell the whole story. Movies and television shed an occasional light on hypnosis, but in most cases skew the facts to intensify fear or intrigue amongst their viewers or present a very limited perspective. Stage hypnotists are very good at generating interest in hypnosis, but their emphasis is on entertainment rather than the therapeutic uses for the tool. And then there are the hypnotherapists themselves, many propagating a limited understanding of hypnosis by only practicing it in very limited ways. Another disturbing trend within the field is for practitioners of hypnosis to call what they do by some other name. Because of the perceived stigma, less controversial terms like guided relaxation, imagery, meditation, visualization and body-mind healing will be used.

It is not my intention to scold or minimize anyone, but rather to provide information. Knowledge is power. And with power comes greater choice. I want to give people more information so that they can potentially make better decisions and perhaps have a better life as a result of those decisions. I also want to challenge hypnosis practitioners to move outside their boxes and tap into the unlimited potential of the mind. I suppose that if I could get only one concept across, it would be that the power of the mind is infinite in its ability to transform our lives. Moreover, it is every individual's right to harness that power to achieve greater self-awareness, control, comfort, vitality, peace, joy, success and so much more. The possibilities are only limited by what people are willing to believe.

Hypnosis is not just for smoking and entertainment. People will only act like a chicken if they want to. No one can make you do something you don't want to do, especially by just having you look into their eyes. Hypnosis may be good for a laugh, but it's good for so much more. The succeeding chapters will attempt to unlock the mystery behind hypnosis and its unending possibilities.

CHAPTER 2

WHAT'S IN A MIND

In order to understand hypnosis and its potential, one must first understand the workings of the mind. Let's begin with an overview of its components.

Think of our minds as one big M&M, a variety of yummy goodness housed inside a protective shell. By the way, have you tried the pretzel filled M&Ms yet? Yum! Anyway, whether you like yours with or without nuts, all minds have a similar framework.

The conscious part of the mind is the section of the mind that functions primarily during our waking hours. It enables us to perform many important tasks related to thinking, such as reasoning, rationalizing, analyzing, calculating, comparing and judging. Judging, in particular, comes from the conscious' need to qualify and quantify everything. It's hot, it's cold, it's good and it's bad. Conscious functions and capabilities come in very handy when we want to balance our checkbook, solve a problem, locate a missing item or discern something. Despite the necessary role that it plays, surprisingly, the conscious is the weakest part of our mind and everything under its jurisdiction is temporary.

The conscious provides a container for memories and information that many consider the location for short term memory. With a limited size and lack of long term or permanent storage capability, it functions more like a staging area. Information of various types and sizes is constantly swapped in and out to help us function in our daily lives. Whether it's the names of people in your life, or the particulars of how to do your job or perform a routine task like driving, or any other piece of information you pick up along the way, the conscious depends upon another part of your mind to hold onto it and then pass it along when you need it.

In addition to temporary memory, the much talked about willpower is yet another resident of our conscious. The very name itself suggests some extent of strength or power. If one believed all the propaganda spouted about willpower, they would think it's the answer to all our problems. Many perceive willpower as some unending well of magic that people can dip into if they are good enough and strong enough. An inability to achieve a goal using willpower often causes people to erroneously believe they are failures, weak, inadequate or lacking control. The truth, however, is that willpower, residing in the very temporary part of the mind, has no lasting power and therefore is incapable of producing long lasting or permanent change.

While some degree of change could result from using willpower, there are no guarantees that it will stick. Willpower is no more than a bandage that stays in place as long as everything is good. For example, people who use willpower to stop smoking may be successful for a while, but if something stressful or emotionally overwhelming comes along, they can easily revert back to their undesired habit. Not because they're bad, weak or undisciplined, but rather because willpower does not address the cause or provide a permanent solution to our issues. Therefore, it is not someone's fault when they fail to realize results using willpower alone.

You may wonder if all our memories do not fit within our conscious and we are unable to use our willpower to make positive permanent changes in our lives, where does that leave us. It leaves us right smack at the entranceway to the subconscious, the real power player in our mind.

Unlike the conscious, the subconscious has unlimited and permanent capacity. Everything that we've ever seen, heard, felt, smelled, touched, expressed, thought or experienced is stored within the subconscious and remains there indefinitely. It is as if someone has followed us around throughout our entire existence recording and documenting everything there is to know about us. Whether one can consciously recall them or not, this wealth of data and memories are safely housed and always accessible. Memories and data stored within the subconscious warehouse are extracted and downloaded into the conscious staging area as needed.

Please indulge me as I describe how I imagine the information exchange that takes place between the two parts of our mind. I envision a large, clear cylindrical pipeline running between the subconscious warehouse and the temporary memory container within the conscious to connect the two. When information is needed, the conscious part of our mind sends a request to the subconscious, much like a manufacturer requests parts from its suppliers. Upon receipt of the request, the subconscious warehouse supervisor delegates to one of its many worker bees to find said item and prepare it for shipment. Dozens of warehouse keepers driving around on high-lows with handheld scanners, search billions of bar-coded shelves, bins and pallets to fill their orders.

Once the items are retrieved from their storage locations, the information is packaged up and loaded into the cylinder. A shipping clerk presses a large silvery button that shoots the parcel through the tube and delivers it into the receiving dock of the conscious. The information is unpacked and available for use. But once the conscious is finished with the information, it is returned to the warehouse for permanent storage. Unlike a traditional order, the whole memory retrieval process occurs in lightning speed.

There are a variety of factors that affect how well we recall past events and data. For one thing, human beings often assign different levels of priority to information and memories they've collected over the years. The ones we like the most are typically given the highest priorities, and those with higher priorities will be easier to recall than those items with lesser priority. The emphasis or lack of emphasis parents place on our childhood memories can also have an effect on memory recall. The more often our parents engage us in remembering, the easier it will be to remember. There are a number of reasons why a person may have difficulty remembering things. Aside from brain injury, toxic interference from drugs and chemicals, inadequate nutrition, hydration or sleep, memory retrieval is usually hampered due to trauma or stress.

A lack of rest, too much to do and too little time to do things, and anything else that puts the body under duress can have the same negative impact on one's mind and memory. Stress can easily make someone forget whether or not they locked their door five seconds ago. If that's not bad enough, there are those frustrating moments when someone knows they know something, but for some reason they are unable to bring the information past the tip of their tongue. When these types of disconnects happen, it's usually a sign that a person is overwhelmed. Better managing one's time, reducing stress factors and incorporating more balance, rest and fun into one's life will make it highly conducive for their memory to return to normal.

While stress can definitely create issues, trauma can be even more detrimental to memory flow. When something bad happens, we have a decision to make. Do we go on as best as we can knowing what happened, or do we forget it? Many people who experience something emotionally disturbing like molestation or abuse, for example, often choose to repress or forget that it ever happened. If they pretend it didn't exist, they believe that it cannot hurt them. Unfortunately, it can. These events are never deleted from the permanent memory of the subconscious. They are simply disconnected from a person's awareness. Like little time bombs, these hidden memories lay in wait until something sets them off. And when that happens, chaos, pain or emotional oozing could manifest without reason or understanding.

To help you understand how this works, think of websites on the internet as different memories we may store within the subconscious. To get to those memories or websites we need a URL or address. When one represses a memory they are essentially throwing away the URL. Without the address, we cannot bring up a website or memory. It still exists and can still affect us, we just don't know about it. This concept causes a great deal of frustration for people who have difficulties in their lives but no explanation for those difficulties. Having to suffer from some pain, depression, anxiety or other undesired manifestation is bad enough, but having no understanding of its origin makes a person think they're crazy too. Thankfully, hypnosis enables us to restore these hidden or missing links to our awareness, so that their associated traumas can be understood, healed and neutralized once and for all.

When a person has full remembrance of their traumas, they will typically come into my office and request that I delete something from their memory that's causing them pain. Knowing that something happened to them is not the problem. The reason why they have an issue is because they still hold an emotional charge regarding the event in question and/or persons involved. If neutralized, a past experience cannot hurt or limit someone anymore, and remembering that it happened will not matter.

For example, when a person has experienced rape, beatings or a terrible accident in their past, the charge of the event generally causes that person to cry and even tremble when speaking about it. After the disturbing incident is neutralized through hypnosis, that same person can relay the details of the event as unemotionally as a person talking about going to the store to get some milk. This is not denial or some delusion. This is real. Feelings of fear, powerlessness, anger, shame or whatever caused them to be limited or discomforted are no longer apart of them. The past is no longer an issue. They are no longer a victim. They are free to be happy and to expect better things for their future.

Before leaving the topic of memory, it is important to recognize that the subconscious is not precise when it comes to shutting off access to memories. Suppose someone had a bad day on September 4, 1987 that they no longer wished to remember. Rather than disconnecting them from that one day's memory, the subconscious will typically select a group of days, weeks or even months that include that particular day. And if there has been recurring trauma over an extended period of time, it is not uncommon for the subconscious to shut out years of a person's life. I've had several clients who could not recall anything that happened to them good or bad, over a span of ten or even fifteen years. And while they had traumas spread across that period of time, it was not continuous.

There were gaps of years where nothing bad had happened, but it was obviously easier for the subconscious to make a big sweeping cut than to individually weed out negative occurrences as they happened.

This brings me to my theory about the frightening condition known as Alzheimer's. At some point in a person's life after having lost a number of people they care about and recognizing that life has become more complicated and maybe difficult, they can make an unconscious choice to block out these painful aspects from their memory. Unfortunately, repressing things can get out of control, and it may seem as though they're living in another place and time. It is extremely common to retreat back to simpler, more comfortable days when everyone they cared about still existed. Tragically, this disconnection is not restricted to memories of people, experiences and discomfort. It could also affect knowledge and abilities that help us cope and more importantly function in life.

It is sad to look at someone who slips away every day bit by bit, and even harder to put yourself in someone else's shoes and understand why they make the choices they do, even unconsciously. I believe these memories can be reconnected. However, I believe most would fight it, even with the knowledge of what the alternative may bring. Sometimes life is too hard.

Before moving on from the topic of memory storage and retrieval, I would like to point out that recall can be improved even if there isn't a problem. Just as exercise can make our muscles work better, there are ways to train the mind to work more efficiently. Hypnosis can be used to expedite recall and enable us to process large amounts of information more easily. Conscious functions beyond memory, such as focus, comprehension, analysis and problem solving can also be enhanced through hypnosis. Students and actors will find these improvements especially beneficial.

In addition to providing a warehouse for our memories and experiences, the subconscious facilitates creative and emotional expression. While the conscious allows us to reason and analyze, the subconscious allows us to dream, conjure and imagine anything and everything. One must imagine something to create it. Stirring music, enchanting works of art, inspiring poetry, compelling films and books, beautiful yet functional architecture, revolutionary medical treatments, timesaving technological advancements and just plain fun would be impossible without the subconscious' gift of imagination.

As you will soon see, the imagination is our most powerful tool for reorganizing and manipulating the contents of the subconscious to facilitate greater wellbeing. It allows us to eliminate a great deal of inner junk in lightning speed. And despite the fanciful quality the imagination adds to the process, by the time one's work is complete it will be more than obvious that something very real has occurred.

Aside from its more creative aspects, the subconscious also allows us to feel and respond to everything we experience. And while emotions like sadness and anger are not typically desirable, joy and love are. Emotion is essential to our ability to be human, and thanks to the subconscious we have a means to express that humanness. The subconscious not only provides a means to express our feelings, but a vehicle to store our emotional response to life experiences.

Other noteworthy residents of the powerful subconscious are habits, patterns, triggers and belief systems. Why and how we view ourselves and our world, as well as why and how we behave and respond to people, places, situations and things, is stored within the unlimited confines of this part of our mind.

While the perceptions, triggers, habits, patterns and emotional responses held within the subconscious may not be known on a conscious level, they can still significantly affect our lives. This will be discussed in future chapters.

An important subcomponent of the subconscious, known as the unconscious, has two primary functions: to act as a repository for past life memories and automatically control body functions and our immune system.

As for being a storage area for past life information, for those who are willing to believe in reincarnation, life lessons, karma and such, it's a wonderful area to tap into to further understand who we are. I will explore some of these aspects later on in the book.

The second function of the unconscious, the control of autonomic responses and immunity is highly important to our staying alive and healthy. Aside from protecting our body from illness, thanks to this part of our mind, things like breathing and having our blood flow through our body are taken care of for us. Unfortunately, when junk piles up in the subconscious, this can cause inefficiencies in the way it runs our body and can make us more prone to ill health. We can use the knowledge of this linkage between our body and mind to remove barriers to good health and improve one's comfort, strength, energy and quality of life. Also, by working with the subconscious, chronic pain and illness can often be reversed even when traditional medical approaches have failed. Unfortunately, because the mind's near unlimited potential for physical transformation is not common knowledge, it isn't taken advantage of as often as it should.

By invoking the imagination during hypnosis, a person can affect virtually every aspect of their physiology. One's heart rate, blood pressure, breathing, body temperature and comfort level, just to name a few, can all be influenced via the subconscious mind. Our spinal column can even be realigned much like a traditional chiropractic adjustment, but by only using our thoughts.

Another significant aspect of the body-mind connection is that through hypnosis one can create an anesthesia or numbing type phenomenon equivalent to chemical induced anesthesia, without the drug related risks. Essentially, while the brain may continue to send pain messages, the subconscious mind can be instructed to ignore them and maintain total comfort despite them. The body can also be programmed to work more cooperatively with medical and dental procedures or surgeries. Hypnosis can help minimize bleeding and complications, maintain normal vital signs, accelerate healing and reduce procedure and recovery times. This same ability can be applied to accelerate the healing of the body after injury.

It is also notable that the body-mind connection can be used to isolate and protect certain parts of the body from the adverse affects of certain medications, as well as treatment protocols such as chemotherapy and radiation. With prior hypnotic preparation, cancer treatments can work with laser-like precision to eradicate unhealthy cells yet keep healthy cells perfectly in tact. This can result in increased survival rates, as well as faster and easier recoveries. For those who find the side effects of certain medications to be intolerable, but would like to take advantage of the benefits they offer, hypnosis offers a means to control what a medicine does and does not do.

As powerful as the subconscious may be, there is a great deal of skepticism as well as curiosity regarding its very existence, along with where it may found in the body. Science can measure changes in our brain when we engage our subconscious during hypnosis, but while it would be easy to think of the subconscious as residing somewhere inside our brains, there is no definitive evidence to prove such a concept. Thus, there is a great deal of speculation regarding its location. Popular opinion holds that the subconscious exists in the right side of our brains because of its response to imagination and other non-analytical aspects typically associated with that side of our brain. But while the subconscious affects brain function along with many other parts of our body, unlike the conscious part of our mind, the subconscious is not truly physical.

   I like to think of the subconscious as an interface or bridge much like a digital converter box connected to a television. The subconscious, residing on another level of existence imperceptible to the physical eye, plugs into the physical level to send and receive information and messages to and from the brain and other parts of our body. It downloads information into our very cells, allowing for cellular memory. Our subconscious also connects to alternative levels of existence and our very soul. Its linkage with other dimensions offers us the ability to communicate with more spiritual or otherworldly aspects such as departed loved ones, guides, guardian angels, ghosts, another person's subconscious, pets and what I call the universal consciousness or collective of all consciousness.

The subconscious knows everything about us. Who and what we like, as well as, whom and what we don't like. It knows what we need more of and what we need less of. It knows what inspires us, what makes us happy, what limits us and what can bring us to our knees. It knows our deepest desires and fears, as well as our greatest victories, failures and disappointments. The subconscious carries all the knowledge and skills we acquire in life. It also stores all of our beliefs, along with our reasons for having them. The subconscious holds the key to why we are the way we are, but more importantly, it holds the promise of change. Through the subconscious, we can transform our body, mind and spirit and fulfill our potential for greater health, comfort, happiness, success and all that is good.

CHAPTER 3

CREATING BELIEFS, PERCEPTIONS & BEHAVIOR PATTERNS

At some undetermined point, while floating around inside the womb of our mothers, our subconscious mind appears on the scene like clean sheets of paper waiting to be written upon. Well, they're not entirely clean. They also hold information related to past lives and karma within their fresh new pages. But we're not going to go into that right now.

In the beginning, the primary job of the subconscious is to take in information and not ask questions. So like a soldier on a mission, it acts like a great big sponge sopping up data, facts, tidbits, language, skills, messages, impressions and emotions with total abandon. It takes in everything we see, feel, hear, touch, smell, do, think, say and sense without judgment or restriction. Something is not good or bad, it just is, at least to the subconscious that is. The conscious part of our mind, on the other hand, is very opinionated as to the good and bad quality of our experiences. It frequently provides a peanut gallery commentary along the way, but has no involvement or choice as to what gets put into the subconscious warehouse.

When a child is developing in the womb, the types of information collected by the subconscious is limited to the environment of the mother and what the mother is feeling, along with what people are saying about the child on the outside. After the child is born, the subconscious is highly focused on gathering all the necessary information to help them walk, talk, read, write and do all the things children do. This explains why children can learn so fast.

The subconscious not only brings in information to document a person's experience and help them function in life, but it also stores their response to it all. One of the most critical responses we have is our beliefs.

Based on our very first experiences, we begin to construct beliefs and perceptions within the subconscious that could eventually have a significant effect on our lives. When I refer to the concept of beliefs and perceptions, I'm not talking about whether a person believes in God or capital punishment, although those beliefs are stored

CREATING BELIEFS, PERCEPTIONS & BEHAVIOR PATTERNS

within the subconscious as well. It is our core beliefs and perceptions that are our primary focus. I'm talking about how we feel about our world and ourselves. Am I good, loved, loveable, worthy, smart, beautiful and strong or am I bad, unloved, unlovable, unworthy, stupid, ugly and weak? Is the world good and safe or is it bad and unsafe? Is life easy or is it difficult?

Our beliefs and perceptions depend upon a variety of factors. The environment in which we grow up will have significant impact on how we feel about ourselves and our world. Those who have the benefit of a stable, loving, nurturing, calm, supportive and dependable environment often feel a high degree of self-worth and confidence as well as security in the world. Others who've had the unfortunate experience of growing up in a critical, unloving, volatile or even violent environment will generally feel unworthy, unloved and unsafe. Keep in mind, the environment around their mother while they are in the womb can impact the child just as significantly as the environment they live in once they get out.

Another factor that can greatly influence our beliefs and perceptions is the toolkit of our parents. Skills and rules that help us move through life and cope are passed down from generation to generation. Among many things, these tools determine how we communicate, express emotion and affection, care for ourselves and cope with conflict. Those who lack tools will not only tend to struggle more, but will find it difficult to cultivate self-worth or a positive outlook in their offspring. Parents lacking self-esteem or self-love will also find it difficult, if not impossible, to show their children how to love themselves having never known what that feels like.

Most mothers and fathers do not set out to hurt or limit their children. Unfortunately, they don't always have the tools necessary to meet our needs or avoid causing harm. Unless a person encounters someone with other tools or has the awareness and initiative to seek out alternatives for themselves, they will ultimately be limited by the ones that were passed onto them. People often blame genetic predisposition for the propensity to experience the same issues as their parents. I think it's more about the fact that generations who use the same limited set of tools to get through life will experience the same undesired results. If you want a different experience, you have to get some better tools and change the way you deal with life.

In addition to the life tools we are given, the messages we receive can also affect what we think and feel about ourselves and our world. I love you. I hate you. You're smart. You're stupid. You can do and be anything. You can't do anything right. You'll never amount to anything, so don't bother trying. You're beautiful. You're ugly. I'm glad you were born. I wish you were never born. I'll love you no matter what. I'll only love you if you're good. Gosh, I hate that last one. There is nothing more

CREATING BELIEFS, PERCEPTIONS & BEHAVIOR PATTERNS

wounding than giving a child the impression that your love for them is conditional.

Before I went onto my soapbox, I was talking about messages we get. The examples I provided earlier are more direct type messages which require little or no explanation of their meaning. There are also indirect messages that we give ourselves based on how we interpret our experiences. Whether or not they have any validity, make no mistake, these indirect messages can impact us just as greatly as the direct ones. The following is an example of a negative indirect message that someone might take in.

Five year old Sam had a very bad day at school. His best friend Max said something mean to him that he just can't seem to get over. Keep in mind that the world of a child is small. When one little thing goes wrong in their world, it can seem like the end of the world. Like most children, Sam thinks this is the end of his world. As such, his ride home from school is long and quiet. Meanwhile, back at home, Sam's parents are dealing with a crisis of their own; his dad just lost his job. Sam's parents are naturally worried and are trying to figure out how they're going to manage to pay all their bills.

The minute Sam arrived at his house, he raced through the door to find his mom and cry to her about his terrible tragedy. Totally focused on their own trauma, his parents dismissed Sam to his room to deal with his upset alone. "Not now" was all they said, but to Sam it was more like never. When he got to his room, Sam threw himself onto his bed and cried. Something awful happened and his parents wouldn't talk to him or comfort him in his time of need. What did this mean?

After giving the matter some consideration, Sam could only conclude that his parents didn't care and that he wasn't very important to them. He figured that if they really cared and thought he was important, they would have stopped whatever they were doing and immediately dealt with his problem. Since they didn't do that, he had no choice but to think the worst. But Sam doesn't stop there. He extrapolates from this theory a new theory that his parents probably never loved him and that they probably wished he was never born. And if your parents do not love or want you, no one else will. Sam therefore comes to the invalid assumption that he is not lovable. This may sound extreme, but I assure you, children make these leaps all the time.

Contrary to Sam's belief, his parents do love him. They were just preoccupied with their own problem at the time. They never said to him that they don't care or love him. He came to that conclusion himself. Later on, when his parents try to talk to him, he doesn't say a thing. Because he's already made up his mind, he sees no point in opening himself up to further disappointment or hurt. Sam will never tell his parents what he suspects about their feelings about him, nor will he scold them on their parenting skills

CREATING BELIEFS, PERCEPTIONS & BEHAVIOR PATTERNS

not meeting his needs. He will just stock away the limited perceptions he built regarding this time in his life and probably forget that it ever happened.

There is one more thing I want to discuss regarding the messages we receive. As I mentioned earlier, while in utero we are fully aware of the state of things around our mothers. As part of that awareness, we can listen in on conversations and music and even delight in loving chatter directed toward our mother's bellies. These potential interactions provide a number of direct and indirect messages that we can take into our subconscious.

Positive messages that reinforce that a child is wanted will build positive perceptions in a developing child's mind. On the other hand, discussions of more negative perspectives such as the consideration of having an abortion will most likely cause a child to store unworthy and unlovable beliefs. Aside from the words they hear in utero, the mood and behavior of their mother during pregnancy can also be potentially detrimental to a person's sense of value, comfort or perception of the world. Unfortunately, in the case where parents have considered an abortion, yet ultimately changed their mind and allowed the pregnancy to come to full term, the damage has already been done. And no matter how much the parents may have grown to love their child, the child may never truly believe it.

CHAPTER 4

GOAL-DRIVEN BORDER GUARD READY FOR DUTY

At around age eight or nine, the unrestricted flow of information in and out of the subconscious comes to an end. From this moment on, the subconscious will take on a more active role in what gets stored. To facilitate its new managerial directive, the subconscious will install a protective barrier at its entranceway. Although it is clinically referred to as the Critical Faculty, I prefer to think of this new player as a border guard on a mission. The objective of this added structure is to lock in all previously stored information, and decide which new ones, if any, should be allowed entry in the future.

The newly appointed border guard must determine whether a new bit of information is compatible with what is already stored within the subconscious before it can permit entrance. If it matches or is similar to what's already there, it can be stored. If however, the new data is incompatible with or unlike any existing information, it will be rejected. When a new piece of information has nothing in the subconscious warehouse to be compared against, it will go in unrestricted and become the basis for future comparisons.

The problem with the Critical Faculty is that its discernment is at too high a level. While it can identify things that are similar, it still cannot determine whether they are good or bad. For example, when looking at two pens, the border guard sees two devices designed to write with and thus views them as being the same. At a high level they are. But if we dig a little deeper, we may discover that one of the pens works, while the other is broken. From a standpoint of use, this is a very important detail. Unfortunately, the Critical Faculty cannot ascertain or measure this distinction, so it will ultimately ignore it.

To demonstrate how this works, I will use two people with almost opposite experiences.

First there's Sally. Sally grew up with loving parents and lots of positive reinforcement and experiences. She feels confident, worthy, loved, smart and good in every way. Sally views the world as a safe and happy place.

Our second person is Joe. Unlike Sally, Joe had an extremely volatile and often abusive early childhood. The messages he received were primarily negative and demeaning. Joe feels insecure, unloved, unworthy and unsafe, and views the world as a dark and difficult place.

Most people do not have such extremely one-sided experiences. More typically, children have both good and bad. I'm using the vast contrast for illustration purposes.

So now with their border guards in place, let's look at what happens when a new piece of information comes their way.

The first person to approach Joe and Sally is Mary. Mary is a very nice girl with only positive things to say to both of them. She emphasizes their good qualities and offers only support, honesty, encouragement and friendship.

Sally's border guard views Mary's messages and treatment as being similar to the ones already stored and easily welcomes the new data inside. The new information combines with the old, strengthening Sally's good feelings about herself and her world. This is good for Sally.

Joe's border guard on the other hand, sees Mary's messages and treatment as being completely out of harmony with what already exists within his subconscious. It has no choice but to reject the good experience and protect and preserve the ill will Joe carries about the world and himself. This is not good for Joe.

Now a new person enters the scenario. His name is Tom. Tom is a very negative person with abusive tendencies. His messages and behavior are intended to intimidate, minimize and promote discomfort.

Sally's border guard determines that Tom's words and actions are unlike anything she has in her subconscious, and therefore disallows its entrance. This act protects Sally's positive feelings about herself and the world. This is very good for Sally.

Unfortunately, Joe's border guard sees a strong similarity between Tom's message and treatment and the beliefs and perceptions Joe already holds. It has no alternative but to let this new information in. The new data will join with the old. This will intensify Joe's negative perspectives and make them more deeply rooted. This is very bad for Joe.

But the Critical Faculty does not stop there. Desiring to be more useful and lacking the patience to wait for something to act upon, the border guard takes on a more active role in the process. The now goal-driven Critical

Faculty will seek out experiences and people that coincide with existing perceptions and beliefs held within the subconscious. Like a magnet, it draws into one's life things that reflect what they were conditioned to believe, not necessarily what they want. This concept is commonly referred to as the law of attraction. Like attracts like. Positive thoughts and feelings attract positive people and experiences, while negative thoughts and feelings draw negative persons and encounters.

Anytime you find yourself experiencing something that is vastly different than what you want, most likely you've stored a belief that makes you feel unworthy of having what you desire. And no matter how much you want something, if you do not believe subconsciously that you should have it, you won't. A perfect example of this type of disconnect or disharmony is with people who want good, supportive, honest, loving, safe and mutually satisfying relationships, but have every self-absorbed, lying, insensitive, user and abuser lining up to be their friend or romantic partner. Another example where the law of attraction is working against someone is in the case of a person who wants to be prosperous and successful, but seems to miss every opportunity to make a buck or get ahead.

As if that's not bad enough, the limiting aspect of beliefs and perceptions can sometimes have a more lethal impact. For example, I had four different clients, unknown to one another, who came to me within the same year to address the same exact set of issues. Each person had a highly compromised immune system, as well as chronic pain, fatigue and illness. All of them had really good people and circumstances in their lives at the time, but were unable to enjoy them because they were always sick. None of them were able to turn things around or get relief no matter what they did. Intriguingly, they all shared commonalities in their past as well.

All of these individuals came from abusive childhoods, both physical and sexual. Each one also experienced a near death illness at an early age. In the midst of their respective health crisis, they all noticed something significant; no one was hurting them. They were also receiving a lot more attention than usual, and every bit of it was positive. During these life and death moments, each person made a choice that would forever alter the rest of their lives assuming that they lived, which they all did. Each one was utterly convinced that it was safer to be unhealthy. They all stored a belief that being healthy wasn't safe. Being a goal driven sort, the subconscious had no choice but to keep them safe by drawing more illness into their lives.

When there are negative perceptions and beliefs, it is easy to feel like the world is against you or that there's a battle between good and evil going on inside of you and you're not winning.

To put a stop to this negative cycle, one must change the very things that are driving it. Through hypnosis, invalid perceptions and beliefs can be rewritten to more positive ones, enabling the goal driven subconscious to work more effectively in someone's behalf.

The rewriting or reprogramming of subconscious perceptions and beliefs is much like downloading a new release or upgrade to a computer to replace outdated inefficient software and provide additional functionality. Not only does everything work better and faster, but in most cases the added tools can be highly beneficial in providing someone with greater opportunity as well as ease in their daily life. With the subconscious now in harmony with the conscious, one's experiences can now reflect what they want, rather than what they were conditioned to accept. And the Critical Faculty will protect these new more positive beliefs and rules for living just as strongly as it did the old undesirable ones.

When the law of attraction is working for someone, their world will seem almost magical. Things that were once a struggle are suddenly easy. Opportunities that were non-existent or distant are now in the forefront and in abundance. Those who previously mistreated them either change or leave, while new people come into their life who are much more positive, honest, balanced, loving and supportive.

As for those previously mentioned clients with poor health, when their invalid belief was corrected, their bodies all began to heal, repair and strengthen themselves. And now they are all very healthy, happy and yet completely safe.

Before going onto the next topic, I need you to know that there's an exception to what I've told you in the last couple of chapters. Despite being exposed to a negative environment and constant stream of negative messages, some people do not take these things personally, but rather choose to ignore them and accept only positive beliefs about themselves. As such, these rare individuals experience the opposite of those from similar backgrounds. How is this possible? I believe that it's due in large part to the unique spirit, wisdom and personality of certain souls, along with their sheer stubbornness and will to continue and even flourish. These traits can cause some people to make choices that those in similar circumstances would not. These very same aspects may cause a person to seek out new tools for living rather than limiting themselves to the ones that their parents gave them.

To exemplify this difference, let's revisit the situation I spoke of earlier regarding children who overhear their parents debate on whether or not to abort them while they're in their mother's womb. As I said before, most children in this situation will store a belief of being unloved and unworthy. On rare occasions though, someone will simply invalidate the declarations of their parents, labeling them as laughable and obviously untrue. They cannot imagine anyone seriously not wanting them, and rather than accepting something negative about themselves, they decide that it is their parents who are flawed. At the very most, these uncommon individuals feel frustration and even pity for their parent's stupidity. What they do not feel is unworthy or unloved. Disaster avoided.

CHAPTER 5

FEELINGS, SO MUCH MORE THAN FEELINGS

We not only create perceptions and beliefs about ourselves and our world regarding our experiences, we also have an emotional response to them. When bad things happen in particular, they make us feel sad, angry, fearful, powerless, betrayed, overwhelmed, or any number of other negative emotions. Feeling bad is not a problem. Ignoring or not expressing those feelings, however, can be a very big problem.

One's environment, upbringing, personality, coping mechanisms and tools are some of the factors that can determine how well we deal with our emotions, and how and if we express them. Those who allow their emotions to flow freely are unfortunately in the minority. Individuals who are emotionally detached or stunted in some way are more prevalent.

Growing up in a home where discussion and expression of feelings is highly discouraged is a common scenario that leads to future repression of emotions. Being the designated rock among loved ones and friends can also result in a disregarding of one's own feelings. Perceiving the expression of emotions to be a sign of weakness will also inevitably hamper one's ability to deal with their feelings as well.

Regardless of the reason, if a person is unable to express their emotions when they occur, their feelings will not simply go away. The goal driven subconscious will store unexpressed negative emotions in various parts of the body for later resolution. As to their specific locations, it will vary by individual.

Some people have their favorite storage spots, like the chest area or the abdominal region. Various emotions also have a strong affinity to certain locations in the body. For example, heartache, loss, grief and sadness in general are highly attracted to the heart and chest. Worry, fear and guilt have a close relationship to the gut area. The neck and/or shoulders are popular storage areas for stress, as well as excessive burden or responsibility. The throat is highly affected by an inability to express one's thoughts, feelings and ideas. And one who is supportive of others, but feels a lack of support in one or more areas of their life, will often store it in their back.

Regardless of the attraction of certain emotions to certain parts of our body, the subconscious can store it anywhere. For example, I once had a client who stored every negative emotion they ever had in their big right toe. The toe was practically hanging by a thread when they came into my office. It had undergone at least five different medical procedures or surgeries over the years. Why the toe? I could not say. Whatever the reason, this was my client's favorite storage location. And when all was said and done, the client felt great and so did their toe.

Aside from storing our own emotional response to our experiences, we are also capable of storing other people's emotions as well. A child, who is still developing in the womb of their mother for example, can store their own mother's fears, sadness, stress or any other negative emotions they might experience during pregnancy. The following case example illustrates this vulnerability perfectly.

A client came to see me who had suffered from unexplainable depression since they were little. Years of traditional therapy and medicine proved ineffectual. Thankfully, hypnosis finally gave this client the answer and relief they always wanted. Months before my client was born, their parents suffered a tragic loss of one of their children. Understandably, their mother was overcome with grief. Unfortunately, her intense sadness became part of her unborn child, and eventually contributed to her newborn's depression. Once the source of their issue was identified and released, my client was able to feel joy and experience the lighter aspects of life.

Regardless of where it came from, what happens after a negative unresolved emotion is stored in the body? This will depend upon a variety of factors including how many negative experiences a person has, along with the volume and intensity of feelings being tucked in. Some emotions can lay in wait for years, while others can take on some sense of urgency within a matter of weeks or months. When the subconscious determines that it has given us plenty of time to resolve our feelings and sees no progress being made, it makes it a priority to get our attention.

The subconscious has only two ways to let us know that something is wrong. The first is through our dreams. They are one of the few windows we have into our subconscious to get a reading on how we think and feel about things in our life. Unfortunately, dreams are often minimized or ignored as some irrelevant piece of entertainment that we endure while sleeping. Despite the vital clues they offer, if dreams are given any measure of consideration, most people find them confusing due to the excessive use of symbolism or convoluted imagery often employed by the subconscious. And even if someone is able to decipher the puzzle of their mind and come up with a reasonable explanation of what's bothering them, there is no guarantee that it will solve the issue.

When someone is plagued by recurring dreams or nightmares, aside from it being a possible reflection of the type of TV shows and movies they're watching, it usually indicates that the subconscious has escalated its efforts to get their attention. These intensely negative or repetitive occurrences are pushing us to address our most troubling issues before they cause us greater difficulty. Sleep walking and sleep eating are also manifestations of unresolved subconscious aspects that may have reached a heightened level. The good news is that if issues are addressed via hypnosis and the subconscious is finally given a voice, there will no longer be any need to bombard our nightly slumber with bad dreams and other unpleasant intrusions.

Aside from facilitating a more peaceful night sleep, hypnosis can also be used to obtain the true meaning of our dreams. And while making personal guesses or searching dream books for interpretations can be both valuable and entertaining, getting it straight from the horse's mouth can be even better.

If the ever vigilant subconscious determines that the dream option isn't working as expected, it will implement plan B. I would like to preface the following information by saying that the subconscious is not against us, nor does it want to kill us. It just doesn't have a lot of tools to work with. Keep this in mind as I elaborate on plan B.

The subconscious recognizes two things, one of which is that human beings do not learn through joy, but rather through suffering. When was the last time you looked for more ways to improve your life when things were going well? The truth is probably never. People do not fix things that are not broken. But when there is chaos, pain or some difficulty, human beings are inclined to seek out help and solutions. The subconscious understands this concept very well.

The second thing the subconscious knows is that it controls our body. And since pain is a big motivating factor, it decides to use its ability to change our physical state to get our attention.

The subconscious will start out small. It might begin for example, by disrupting our ability to sleep or triggering a headache, some indigestion, back pain or some other minor discomfort or ailment. The typical response for someone with these issues would be to take a pill, rather than to attribute this occurrence to something emotional. Failing to get its message across, the subconscious will try a different tack.

Presuming that quantity and repetition are keys to success, the subconscious makes symptoms less isolated and more frequent. Suddenly, one loses sleep or has a headache, indigestion or back pain for five days in a row. This does get our attention. But again, our thoughts are not focused on the emotional component of this upsetting manifestation. After all, it is physical. However, there is no germ, toxin, smack to the head, or other external aspect causing it. So like a typical human being, the person in pain goes to a doctor.

Generally, a doctor will simply give them a stronger pill and tell them to be glad they don't have cancer. Their patient is glad they don't have cancer, and gratefully takes their stronger pill and hopes for the best. But the problem continues.

The subconscious will persist in its efforts to help us recognize we have unresolved negatively charged emotions to deal with. It will continue to use our dreams, along with breaking down our immune system to cause further discomfort, illness and even disease in our bodies. Again, this is not because it wants to hurt us, but because it wants to help. The subconscious just has no tools.

If a person finally expresses an emotion, it can come out in an exaggerated or less reasonable form. Tucking in our emotions builds up a pressure akin to water in a tea kettle coming to a boil on a hot stove. There is just so much we can take before we have to let out some steam, so to speak. One incident, big or small, can be the straw that breaks the camel's back and the catalyst for emotional overflow.

When a person responds in an extreme way such as screaming like a crazy person or throwing or breaking something after something minor occurs, it is important to recognize what's really happening. It's not about that moment, but rather all the other moments that came before it that made that person angry, moments, he or she could not express or come to peace with. Combined, they become an over-response called rage. Just like anger can transform into rage, the unshed tears of sadness can grow into depression, and little fears and worries can pile up and become a full blown panic attack.

Post traumatic stress disorder (PTSD) is a well known manifestation of too much trauma and insufficient outlets for emotional expression. But instead of just one exaggerated emotional response, there are many. PTSD may encompass depression, anxiety, rage, insomnia, nightmares, violent flashbacks, relationship issues as well as other life limiting aspects, all at the same time.

Soldiers, police officers and other men and women of service that are exposed to regular violence and trauma are particularly susceptible to future emotional issues. In order to perform effectively at their job and to minimize injury or death, they have to do what I call "doing the drill." Any fear, shock, sadness and even anger they experience during their time on the job must be suppressed until some more convenient and potentially safer point in the future.

Succumbing to the emotions of the moment could cost someone their life. People who serve to protect others generally cannot even risk taking a moment to mourn the loss of a fallen comrade. And so they tuck all their feelings in and perform like machines instead of the human beings they truly are. Even during brief periods of calm and quiet, they are careful not to go to the dark emotions they have hidden so well, for fear they will never be able to go back to doing the drill. But then it's finally time to come home, where there is no enemy to fight and no back to watch. Unfortunately, it's also time to pay the piper and their teapots runneth over.

If we can find these negatively charged emotions and give them a way out, the physical symptoms they created generally go away and many of the illnesses or diseases caused by them can often be reversed. The body can revert itself back to a healthier more comfortable state and thus provide someone with a higher quality of life. Aside from physical improvements, one will also experience greater emotional stability and wellbeing. Future emotional responses will also be more manageable and appropriate for the situation, and easier to get over.

To release emotions in a traditional way, one would have to engage in a full on emote-fest to let them all out. Whether they cry hysterically, tell everyone they encounter what they think, write scathing notes, yell and scream, destroy property, beat people up or shriek with terror, it could take many years to free someone of all their emotional baggage. This option is highly impractical and uncomfortable. It also relies upon a person being fully aware of all the emotions they've been repressing. A more efficient approach is to use hypnosis to find and release these aspects.

With hypnosis, huge chunks of unresolved negatively charged emotions can be neutralized and eliminated within a matter of seconds or minutes. The result will be a significant uplifting and lightening effect without the overwhelm or excessive passage of time typically associated with traditional emotional expression.

I think it's important to mention, before we go on, that one of the best things a person can do for themselves is to express their feelings. Alone or with someone else, talk about it, write about it, cry, curse, yell, punch a pillow, watch a movie, read a book or listen to music that evokes the same feelings. Just do whatever is necessary to get it out. Well maybe not everything. I'm certainly not suggesting that one commit a crime or injure someone or themselves in order to get some release. There are many safe and constructive ways of accomplishing the same effect. If you choose to ignore these feelings, however, they will come out when you least expect it, and trust me when I say, it will not be pretty or nearly as easy.

CHAPTER 6

BLOCKAGES, BUTTONS & TRIGGERS OH MY!

Negative experiences, beliefs and limiting perceptions, along with unresolved negative emotions, provide a fertile ground for the development of a multitude of buttons, triggers, blockages and other undesired manifestations that can wreak further havoc on our lives. Again, the subconscious does not intend to hurt us. It wants to help. Unfortunately, it doesn't have many positive ways in which to get the job done.

When activated either by other people or ourselves, buttons and triggers can cause a wide range of undesired responses, behaviors and discomforts. Examples of what can result from these subconscious troublemakers include: mood swings, bad tempers, nervousness, habits, addictions, sleeplessness, reduced focus, motivation and memory, fears, phobias, obsessive compulsive behaviors, lying, cheating, impulsiveness, stealing, self-doubt, self-sabotage and pain. Hypnosis allows us to deactivate their influence and gain greater control over our own responses and comfort.

The buttons and triggers created by the subconscious can also give rise to blockages and walls that can have varying degrees of impact on one's life. Examples of this are: wanting a promotion, but not being able to get one no matter how hard you work; wanting to move to another state, but being unable to sell a house or find a job in one's dream location. A goal, a dream or a desperate need, seemingly unattainable no matter what you do, could be a barrier created by your subconscious to help you address some unresolved aspect.

Imagine for example, dozens of apple trees, overflowing with ripe fruit, lining both sides of a winding country road. Now imagine a horse traveling along that road desperately craving apples. Unfortunately, this horse has blinders on and is unable to see the delicious offerings all around him, and ends up going hungry. Like a horse with blinders, the subconscious can create blockages that can prevent us from seeing the opportunities that can provide for our needs and desires.

In an effort to help us, the subconscious can reduce one's options and make it seem as if the walls are closing in and there is no perceivable way out. But in truth, there is a way out. With hypnosis, we can find and release these blockages along with the things that contributed to them being created in the first place. Once gone, opportunities will seem to sprout from everywhere and everything will feel possible once again.

While most blockages are erected to hinder aspects external to a person, barriers can also be created to obstruct or limit change and healing or even prevent connection to the subconscious itself. When a client has difficulty getting into a hypnotic state, obtaining information or releasing negative aspects while in hypnosis, they are commonly classified as being resistant. While most people do not like to be uncomfortable or have difficulty in their life, no one typically relishes the idea of facing their problems or making changes. People get very comfortable with what is familiar, even if it isn't always comfortable. Sometimes the potential pain of changing seems greater to a person than the pain of staying the same. And even if a person says they're open to change, a part of them may not be completely onboard with the idea.

The biggest contributing factor to resistance is fear. Fear of the unknown. Fear of losing control. Fear of being happy. Fear of failure. Fear of success. Fear only has power if we give it power. One needs to let go of their fears in order to experience the change they desire. Another major cause of resistance is disbelief in one's ability to change or get better. Doubts are normal and can be overcome. If, however, someone lacks even the slightest hope of alleviating or resolving their issue, it is highly unlikely that they will ever be able to experience any change, let alone the hypnosis state. The final source of resistance is the hardest to accept, but I assure you it happens all the time. Some people prefer to suffer or remain the victim, so they can get attention or continue to blame others for their circumstances.

    Most resistance can be fought with choice and a bombardment of intention, prayer and commands directed to the subconscious. I've spent many sessions waging war dressed in invisible armor and boots, wielding imaginary weapons, and most of all using every bit of creativity, intuition and downright sneakiness to coax each subconscious nemesis into cooperation and lead my clients to victory. Unfortunately some battles cannot be won. The sad truth is that not everyone can be fixed or really wants to be fixed. And as difficult as that may be, we all need to respect where others are in their journey and most of all remember we are only responsible for ourselves. Thankfully, though, there are many who do want transformation. And you know what they say, when we are ready, the universe will provide. And believe me, it does.

Aside from resistance, there is another phenomenon that could impact the progress one makes in their hypnosis work that I feel is worth talking about. While blockages, discomforts and other undesired manifestations are often eliminated once they are identified, the subconscious could choose to initiate a power play that may cause problems to continue. Why would this happen?

When a person's subconscious feels that its concerns are not being taken seriously or acted upon in the best way, it may hold back relief until something changes. If the subconscious used pain as a mechanism to get someone's attention before, it will continue to use this option.

For example, those who sacrifice their comfort, happiness or security for others or fail to express their feelings in a critical matter could feel pain. Someone who doesn't make time to relax and rest when they're overwhelmed or tired could also feel pain. If a client has positively transformed an aspect of themselves or their life, but continues to stay in an uncomfortable environment or surround themselves with negative individuals, they could continue to feel pain.

The subconscious will persist in its efforts until my client can set better boundaries, be more expressive, incorporate more balance in their lives, and demonstrate greater commitment to their own comfort, happiness and security. Once noticeable progress has been made, the subconscious will finally release and deactivate all residual negative aspects and associated triggers.

Keep in mind, the subconscious can withhold final manifestation of any type of change, not just physical, if it feels a client is not doing what they need to do. An interesting example of this kind of power play involves a college-aged client who suddenly experienced a significant reduction in their sports performance. This is the very same sport that afforded them a generous scholarship in their college of choice.

This person went from being top of their game and ripe for a professional career in their sport, to non-functioning. Novices were playing better than this individual. Not only did this client have the pressure of having to perform at a certain level to keep their scholarship, but they also had pressure coming from their father and mother. Unsurprisingly, my client was feeling quite anxious and defeated when they came to see me.

Results do not typically manifest instantly or dramatically. Most clients experience gradual improvements as they move through their work. However, to the supreme frustration of my client, nothing seemed to budge even after three sessions. When I queried their subconscious for some explanation, initially there was some hesitation to give us an answer. Thankfully, after pressing the issue again, their subconscious finally told us what was causing the hold up.

This client had absolutely no desire to go pro, at least not at the present time. But expectations were high around them and pressures were building to put them on the fast track. They weren't ready for the commitment that would be required and just wanted to enjoy their college experience like everyone else. They also had other career aspirations and had no interest in making a profession of their sport. While they were willing to leave their options open for the future, they could not see themselves committing to something this demanding early on in their life. But their parents wanted them to go pro and made it clear that they would be angry and disappointed if their child didn't at least try. Needless to say, my client was terrified to tell their parents the truth.

As long as there was an expectation for them to go pro and an unwillingness for my client to honor their true feelings, their subconscious was determined to block their ability to play well. Unless my client confronted their father and mother and was released from an obligatory professional path, their sport was destined to be sabotaged. Once they made the courageous leap to discuss the situation with their parents, my client was once again able to perform at a high level in their sport and fulfill the requirements of their scholarship.

As you can see, the subconscious will do whatever it thinks is necessary to help you help yourself. If you listen to and follow your heart, most likely you'll avoid that unpleasant scenario when your subconscious takes out the two-by-four to get your attention.

CHAPTER 7

IT'S A HABIT

Habits come in all colors, shapes and sizes. They can be good and they can be bad. Unfortunately, when a habit gets really out of control, they can be nearly impossible to break.

So, what is a habit? Simply put, a habit is something one does with automatic regularity or routine, a patterned response or behavior, if you will, that develops over time. Anything you do at least once a day for a minimum of thirty consecutive days will become a habit. Despite the many attempts to minimize habits and point fingers of blame at the people who have them, a habit is not a small matter that can be easily remedied. Something significant occurs within our bodies to ingrain that behavior or response into our lives. Our brain rewires itself to form a neurological pathway to accommodate every habit we create.

The most common approach for eliminating a habit is to refrain from doing the undesired activity or behavior for at least once a day for a minimum of thirty days, so that the brain can rewire itself and create a new neurological pathway that excludes the habit.

We create habits in virtually every aspect of life, work, play, learning, communication, eating, sleeping, relationships, you name it. Habits are everywhere, and as I said, they can be good or bad. Habits can also be created with or without some emotional complexity or trigger mechanism, and may or may not also have a physical element such as a chemical dependency. Most habits have some degree of emotional complexity, triggering and/or physical aspect or need. Very few do not.

A common phenomenon across college campuses serves as one of the few examples I can think of for a basic habit that has no emotional complexity, triggers or physical reliance. Pretty much every college boy and girl learns to stay up late every night and sleep late every morning. Typically, there is no emotional reason or complex trigger mechanism causing these students to stay up too late and not get up early in the morning. Regardless of how it began, once they graduate and gain employment, their

IT'S A HABIT

sleep habit becomes an urgent problem. Mainly because most companies prefer their employees to arrive at a reasonable time in the morning and be able to function. Thankfully, with relatively small effort, these individuals can adjust their sleep schedule and build new habits to allow them to fall asleep at a reasonable time, awaken at a reasonable time and function more effectively on the job.

Unfortunately, habits that fill some emotional void or have complex trigger mechanisms or some physical element are more difficult to overcome.

A popular avenue for the subconscious is to activate an addictive response for a particular habit. Suddenly, one drink every so often becomes one drink a week, then one drink a day, then several drinks every day with an inability to go without one even for a few hours. While people who develop an addiction often seek out help, they normally address only the physical aspect of their addiction. Their focus will be on removing the undesired substance from their body and distancing themselves from it in the future. If it was really just about chemical dependency, the minute a substance was out of a person's system, they wouldn't need or want it anymore. When a person still has difficultly doing without something, obviously something else is contributing to their addiction.

Addiction is not only driven by physical dependency, but is often created to fill some emotional void. A physical substance or action may calm a person, numb them of pain, give them confidence or courage, or provide some other service that is perceived to be helpful even if it's only temporary. Having this kind of relationship with a chemical or behavior can make it very difficult to give up. And if you never get at the reason why you have an addiction, you cannot truly eliminate it from your life. This is precisely why so many people find themselves in and out of rehab programs.

If a person can refrain from an addictive substance or negative behavior for a minimum of thirty days, despite its complexities, their brain will rewrite itself and create a new neurological pathway that excludes the undesired response. Unfortunately, if they do not address the reasons for their habit or addiction, deactivate its triggers and fill the void it leaves in a positive way, old undeleted pathways and associated undesired habits or addictions can be reactivated at a future date.

With hypnosis however, one can identify the source of the addiction or undesired habit, deactivate its triggers and fill the voids it serves with more positive healthy coping mechanisms. Once the root cause is addressed, old undesired pathways can finally be deleted and new positive habits can take over. The addiction or undesired habit can be eliminated once and for all.

Self-hypnosis CDs are often used to override and disable negative habits, behaviors and responses and ultimately create more positive ones. Listening to a CD at least once a day for a minimum of 30 consecutive days will make the suggestions used in the recording a habit. The subconscious knows if a person requires this kind of reinforcement, so I always ask. This helps me give clients what they need for lasting change.

Before leaving this topic, I do want to mention that unless a person wants to stop doing whatever it is that they are doing either out of habit or addiction, they will not stop. The first step for change is to accept that there is a problem. The second more important step is a willingness and cooperative attitude to do what's necessary to eliminate the undesired habit or addiction from their life. Coercing or even dragging someone in to get help will often result in failure, because the person is not ready to change. Sadly, many people require hitting a major low in their life to feel any motivation to face what they need in order to overcome their issues.

When someone has an addiction, it is important for their family members and friends to not take it personally. People do not typically become an addict or stay an addict to punish those around them. An addicted person is wounded and without adequate tools to cope in life. An addictive substance or behavior can give someone a false sense of control over their pain even if it's only temporary. Friends and loved ones of an addicted person need to set healthy boundaries for themselves, but should be careful not to cast blame or judgment. People who suffer from an addiction already feel bad enough. Telling them that they are bad or selfish for having an addiction is not going to solve the problem. Unfortunately, only when an addictive person finds the courage to face their inner demons can their nightmare come to an end.

CHAPTER 8

OTHER ODDITIES WE STORE

There are a variety of mysterious complaints that have aspects beyond beliefs, habits, triggers, blockages or unresolved emotions. Sometimes the subconscious stores something else to add to the complexity of our issues.

Do you remember when I said that we can store our emotional response to our negative experiences and the blockages they create in our life? Well, we can also store other things about those events that in retrospect seem less obvious or less of an issue. For example, we can store the temperature of our body during the time of upset or trauma.

A former client of mine, who suffered from anxiety and bouts of panic, also experienced periodic night sweats that were so bad that the bed and everything around them would be drenched when they awakened. Doctors were unable to pin down their source, so I made a note to check into it. When I queried this client's subconscious as to the source of their anxiety and panic, we were directed back to a time when they were a child. The event in question caused this client a great deal of fear and worry. In addition to storing the fear and worry they experienced, the client also stored the excessively hot temperature of the day, which was over one hundred degrees.

As I mentioned earlier, the subconscious tries to communicate with us during our dreams to help us to become aware of our unresolved issues. During this client's dream state, their subconscious would trigger the fear and worry they experienced in the past, along with the heat associated with that trauma. Put it all together and you have massive sweating during sleep. Once we released the fear and worry, along with the temperature associated with it, the client was able to sleep through the night and awaken every day feeling calm and cool as a cucumber.

When a person experiences a trauma that includes some physical aspect such as an automobile accident, beating, rape, gunshot or fire, in addition to the emotional charge of that event, they will most likely store a physical element to their trauma. These physical factors can trigger pain, slow or even prevent healing, and even become a catalyst for illness.

One example of this would be someone who suffers from phantom limb pain. Even though a leg may not exist anymore on a physical level, the physical trauma experienced by that leg still lives on one or more levels imperceptible to the physical eye. The negative aspects carried in these energetic templates can then manifest physically. Similar to repressed memories, these hidden elements can cause trouble and pain without understanding or explanation. The good news is that once these physical traumas are released along with their associated emotional aspects, the pain goes away.

Another example of this type of phenomena involves someone who escaped a burning building. Though several years had passed, this person still suffered from sporadic choking sensations and frequent bouts of respiratory ailment. Most people would just conclude that the smoke they inhaled that terrible day did damage to their lungs and that there is nothing that can be done for them. I've had multiple clients with the very same issue and each one of them now breathes perfectly and no longer endures any choking or respiratory illness. Each of them stored the physical and emotional trauma associated with having to escape a fire, along with the actual smoke around them. Yes, they stored the smoke on another level of their being. When we released the physical and emotional trauma of the event, along with the smoke, all their issues went away. As if that wasn't weird enough, in more than one of these cases, I smelled smoke at the time of their release. Cool, huh?

Okay, here's one more example of some of the oddities we store. This one has a past life connection. I've had several clients with unexplainable discomforts and/or unusual markings in certain areas of their body. At some point in my work with each of them, a past life memory was identified by their subconscious as something that was still blocking them. This is not unusual. It was also revealed to them that they suffered some injury or fatal blow of some kind during said lifetime. Maybe a spear to the chest, an arrow to the arm, a musket ball to the thigh, a sword slice to the gut, you get the picture. This also is not unusual. The unusual aspect was that these damaged areas were also coincidentally in the same locations where unusual markings or unexplained discomforts occurred in the person's current life. Also interesting was when we released the physical and emotional trauma from those past life wounds, not only did the discomfort go away, but in most cases, the marks disappeared as well. Extra cool, huh?

I know I said that my previous example was my last example, but I have one more to share, which involves trauma associated with surgery. I've encountered this situation on multiple occasions. The following is just one example.

A client came to see me to address their anxiety and stress. During the course of our initial consultation, they also expressed a desire to find some pain relief in a certain area of their body. The area in question was the site of a recent surgery, which according to their doctor was properly healed and should have no reason to hurt. But it did hurt. I told my client I would look into it.

After resolving the client's other issues, I then directed their subconscious to give us the source of this discomfort. My client was suddenly transported back to the day of their surgery. At some point during the procedure, the doctor felt unsure about something. The surgeon's uncertainty escalated to extreme fear and doubt and a number of other negative emotions. There was even a point where the doctor considered that he might not be able to fix the problem. Just when hope was fading fast, the doctor had a brainstorm and quickly implemented his idea, ultimately resulting in a successful surgical outcome.

How do I know all this you ask? I know this, because every thought and emotion this doctor had was perceptible to my client and also ultimately stored by my client in the area of incision. Even though the surgery was successful, their body wasn't convinced. Once we released these traumatic aspects from their body, their pain went away.

Because my client was horrified by the influence of their surgeon's state of mind in their most recent surgery, they asked me to check on a surgery they had many years earlier.

The experience was the complete opposite of their latest encounter. There was no trauma to lift or problem to rectify. The doctor in charge was confident in his abilities and most of all he had a deep desire to help. My client was awe inspired by the feeling of love, well wishes and support pouring into them during their entire surgery. They told me it felt so good, they could stay like that forever.

This whole scenario brings to light the extreme vulnerability of the subconscious while under anesthesia. Anything that's said, done and felt by the medical staff can not only be perceived and felt by their patient, but it could also affect their ability to heal. Unfortunately, it could also make a difference between whether a person lives or dies. I would also have to add that this applies to people in a coma state as well.

CHAPTER 9

WHAT IS HYPNOSIS?

So now you know how the subconscious works and how and what type of junk gets stored in it. The question now becomes, how do you bypass the Critical Faculty to find out what's going on behind the scenes and make desired changes? It's elementary my dear Watson, HYPNOSIS.

When we are awake, we have the ability to communicate and analyze information, but we are restricted from access to our subconscious.

When we are asleep, our border guard is down and the subconscious is fully accessible. However, one must become lucid and recognize they are dreaming and have the objectivity, self-compassion and skills to work with their subconscious, and oh by the way, not wake up in the process. This approach is difficult at best.

As I've mentioned in an earlier chapter, when the body is in a state of coma or under anesthesia, the subconscious is also accessible. Although there are case studies where an individual has positively affected their healing and recovery while in coma, I truly hope none of my readers experience a health crisis that brings them into such a state regardless of its ability to connect on a subconscious level.

A preferable means to get the job done with a reasonable degree of control and efficiency is to create an altered state of consciousness that blends the best of these worlds. Hypnosis provides the accessibility of the subconscious found during sleep, coma or anesthesia with the awareness and communication capability of someone who is awake.

The act of getting someone into a hypnotic trance is called an induction. There are countless ways to induct or instruct a person into hypnosis. Some use just their voice to coax someone into trance, while others may incorporate objects or physical gestures into the process. Whether or not they use extraneous items or movements to bring their clients into hypnosis, practitioners of the tool typically speak in very soft and almost rhythmic tones to promote relaxation. They will also evoke a person's imagination, given its origins within the subconscious.

Some hypnosis practitioners favor short inductions, while others prefer more lengthy ones.

Rapid or instant inductions, most commonly used in stage shows, typically employ shock, distraction or an offsetting of a person's equilibrium as a means to bypass the Critical Faculty. Startling or confusing the conscious gives a hypnotist a moment of diversion to deliver a short message to the subconscious. In the case of stage shows, the word "sleep" is often used to initiate the dialogue. The effect can be quite dramatic.

Longer inductions, more typical in therapeutic settings, generally utilize a more progressive or gradual relaxation to facilitate accessibility of the subconscious.

There are many opinions in the field, as to which approach is best. Fans of rapid or instant inductions argue that their approach gives the hypnosis practitioner more time to work with the client on their issue. This may be true, as long as the client responds to a quicker induction. Many people are highly stressed and have difficulty relaxing. Longer inductions tend to work best in these cases. Slower inductions also allow clients to become more aware of their bodies and how to relax them at home when they need it. I prefer using longer ones for this very reason. I also believe longer inductions feel less mysterious or manipulative to the subject and thus contribute to greater cooperation and acceptance of hypnosis.

THE HYPNOSIS I KNOW

The following represents one explanation of how a hypnotic trance state may be achieved.

The first step of any induction is to obtain consent. Without it, there should be no hypnosis. No one should force their will upon another person. Choice is at the very heart of any therapeutic modality, especially hypnosis. To be truly successful, one must want to make changes, be ready and willing to face whatever is necessary to achieve those changes and cooperate with the process. It's also beneficial to have a positive attitude going in and some degree of belief in one's ability to change.

Once consent is given, a person's focus must be narrowed. In olden days, a dangling pocket watch was used to bring someone's attention to a single focus and tire their eyes. Later on, a swirling disc or psychedelic image that morphed with some regularity provided a flashier means for realizing the same affect. Although effective, these methods promote more negative perceptions of hypnosis. It is highly beneficial to use less hokey means to narrow focus if you want to be taken seriously. Having someone simply focus on their breathing and/or the voice of the hypnosis practitioner is generally sufficient for achieving the desired result.

As attention is narrowed, one must also clear their mind of thoughts, worries, to-do lists, and other extraneous distractions. To facilitate more relaxation and less mind chatter, the hypnosis practitioner will evoke a client's imagination. The imagination does two things. It keeps the conscious part of the mind busy and distracted while the body is encouraged to slow down and relax. It also helps plug us into the subconscious, because it comes from there. Having a client picture themselves on a beach or walking along a garden path are just a few examples of imagery that can be employed for this purpose. Enlisting all senses during this process can also add to the effectiveness of imagery (i.e. the warmth of the sun, the fragrance of flowers, the sounds of birds and water). As the mind clears and becomes more focused and the body relaxes, brain waves start to slow down. Slower brain waves provide a vital key to unlock the door into the subconscious.

Brain waves are slow when we sleep and more rapid when we are awake. We only need to slow our brain waves down just a little from their waking level to pop open the protective barrier of our subconscious and create a dialogue for change. Once this occurs, information can flow freely. Answers to our most important questions, as well as the feelings we have about them, are right there on the surface, ready to be accessed and communicated without guesswork or hesitation. It will feel like someone has handed you a gigantic folder containing everything about you. Then through some magical invisible device which indexes everything in the folder, you can have almost instant recall of information related to virtually any question you have about yourself.

The subconscious provides us with information by utilizing a combination of our senses. We can see, feel, hear, smell and even think or know something while in hypnosis.

Because hypnosis practitioners are not mind readers, they rely completely on their clients to tell them what the subconscious is presenting to them, regardless of the form it comes in. The hypnotherapist will then give instructions back to the person and their subconscious or request additional information. The preferred language and primary tool for extracting and modifying contents stored within the subconscious is the imagination. Although many times it may feel as if you are simply awake with your eyes closed and making things up in your head, the insights that come to you and the changes you experience as a result of them, will help you recognize that something significant and real has happened.

Many clients are often surprised by how strongly they resonate with or respond to certain thoughts, feelings and memories that rise to the surface, especially ones they don't typically labor upon. And as these pieces are better understood and neutralized through hypnosis, the client experiences a sense of peace and resolution that could not be obtained otherwise. The proof ultimately lies in the results. Any attempt to dismiss or invalidate the existence of this alternative state will fail when one has successfully transformed an aspect of their self or life with it.

Contrary to what movies and stage shows may imply, a person in hypnosis is not asleep or in some vegetative or coma-like state. A hypnotized subject is totally aware of everything that's going on around them at all times, yet they will not be distracted or bothered by any of the external aspects that they are aware of. While in hypnosis, one feels very relaxed, but is perfectly capable of carrying on a conversation. A person does not leave their body when in a state of hypnosis. Therefore, there is no risk of never coming back. Although many wish to linger in this relaxing state, everyone eventually returns to normal consciousness. People often experience a total disconnect from and distortion of time while in hypnosis, leaving them surprised by the time that went by while they were in trance. Upon returning to an awakened state, one will generally feel as if they've had a restful nap.

Clients will remember their hypnosis experience, unless someone instructs them not to. Stage hypnotists often give their volunteers a post hypnotic suggestion (something they are to do when conscious) and then tell them to forget what they told them, for the purpose of getting a laugh. For those people seeking more therapeutic hypnosis, it makes no sense to tell them to forget their experience. Please keep in mind that the will of the client can override a forget instruction and enable them to remember what happened despite being told not to.

With respect to the will of a client, I think it's important to address the greatest misconception about hypnosis regarding control. Many people are under the impression that one relinquishes their power and choice while in hypnosis and can be made to do something they would not ordinarily do. The truth is that I cannot put someone into a trance or keep them in a trance without their consent or cooperation. I cannot force a person to violate their morals or values, or do something they are not willing to do. I cannot make someone change or take a suggestion if they do not want to.

With respect to stage shows, it is important to recognize that people are not being dragged out of the audience against their will. Hypnotists are selecting volunteers who are receptive to the experience and want to let their inhibitions down in order to have some fun. Despite their openness, if at any point a hypnosis subject is asked to do something that they do not want to do, you can rest assure they won't.

The extent of control that a subject has while in hypnosis is so great; they can lie or withhold information. Obviously, that would make helping them difficult, but they can do it. Rather than taking away control, hypnosis can give one greater control in their life by helping them reclaim their power from negative experiences. Of course, they have to want to change and cooperate with the process in order for that to happen.

I probably should mention that there are a few exceptions to what I've said about control. If a person is tortured, threatened, sleep and food deprived, and simultaneously exposed to extreme conditioning, there is a possibility of breaking someone's will or desire. It would be very difficult, but it is possible. Keep in mind, these circumstances are highly unusual and definitely not part of traditional therapeutic hypnosis practice.

Another potential instance of risk involves unethical people who attempt to manipulate situations to encourage people to do things they would not want to do. In this scenario, a person would first have to gain their intended victim's trust and convince them to go into a trance for some positive reason. While in trance, the unethical person could then play on their subject's fears and suggest, for example, that the client's loved one is in danger and that the only way to keep them safe is do whatever they are asking them to do. The awareness one has during hypnosis, combined with the protective mechanisms built into our mind, along with just plain intuition, would cause most people to suspect some manipulation and come right out of trance. It would take a lot for an unethical person to convince their client that they are telling them the truth and affect some manipulation, but it is possible.

There is another vulnerability that I would like to discuss which involves the power we give to others. Some people refer to this as waking hypnosis. We are taught from an early age to respect, believe and listen to authority figures like parents, doctors, teachers, religious leaders and police. And while that may be a good idea most of the time, it's important to realize that they are still human, and as humans, they can make mistakes and say and do inappropriate things.

The power of influence of authority figures is great. They can use this power for good or they can cause great damage with it. By believing in others to an extreme degree, we allow them the ability to bypass our Critical Faculty and lay suggestions directly into our subconscious. When someone puts another human being up on a pedestal, they are giving them the power to enhance or diminish their self-worth, health and comfort, ability to succeed, and even their will to live. A teacher, who tells a student that he or she is stupid or cannot do something, can block that person for their whole life. A doctor who tells a patient it's hopeless and that they're going to die may unknowingly be ensuring their demise. On the other hand, a faith healer can have a positive influence on someone's health or comfort if the audience member believes that person really does have the power to heal.

My advice to everyone is to recognize everyone is human, including the people we are told to look up to.

WHAT IS HYPNOSIS?

Listen to what your heart and gut tell you, not what someone else says or believes. As for authority figures, be very careful of what you say and please do not abuse the power you've been given.

Now that I'm off my soap box, let's talk about the various depths or degrees of hypnosis one can experience. Hypnosis trances that are closer to the conscious or waking state afford easier communication, and thus make it easier for the hypnosis practitioner to get more information and make changes. If however, a person becomes too conscious, information flow could become difficult or stop altogether.

With deeper levels of hypnosis that are closer to the sleep state, information would still be available, but one could become easily distracted and more inclined to drift rather than communicate. There is also a high risk of falling asleep. Extremely deep states of hypnosis are best suited for delivering suggestions for change to the subconscious. To gain understanding of issues and release their cause, lighter trance states are more feasible.

A person's brain waves and trance depth can easily fluctuate during hypnosis. A competent hypnotherapist will manage their client's trance by deepening or lightening it as necessary, to ensure an optimal experience. If for example, a client suddenly has no answers for the questions that are being asked of them, most likely they've become too conscious. Once the hypnotherapist deepens their relaxation, answers can come more easily. On the other hand, if a client seems to be drifting or losing focus, or is taking a lot longer to respond or complete tasks, most likely they've gone too deep. The hypnotherapist would then instruct their client to come up a few notches so they can communicate better and move through the work more quickly. Managing trance depth is also important for insuring that hypnotic suggestions are most effective.

Aside from the traditional means of inducing a hypnotic state, there are a few alternative approaches I believe are worth mentioning before moving on to another topic.

Bringing one to a still point or temporarily pausing someone's brain rhythms via Cranial Sacral Therapy is a great way to get someone who does not easily relax into a hypnotic trance. Once the still point occurs, the person can be coaxed into deepening their trance and initiating a dialogue with the subconscious.

Brushing or manipulating the energetic fields that surround our physical bodies is another potential vehicle for bringing about a trance state. Repetitive sweeping type motions performed above the body with someone else's hands or maybe magnets, as well as a variety of other energetic based healing techniques can move some people into hypnosis. Therapeutic massage can also initiate an altered state and make someone susceptible to emotional releases and other subconscious related manifestations.

CHAPTER 10

HYPNOSIS IS NATURAL

Many people think of hypnosis as being mysterious or illusive and only possible in a stage show or hypnotherapist's office. The truth is hypnosis is a natural state we go into on a regular basis. Given my description of the normal way in which someone can be inducted into a hypnotic trance, you're probably wondering how this could occur without you being aware of it. You are aware of it. You just don't know what to call it. Each of the following scenarios illustrates regular daily occurrences of hypnosis and the opportunities and vulnerabilities they present to us.

A common way in which people can enter a hypnosis trance is by using television as a form of relaxation. The person desiring relaxation gets into a comfortable position. As they begin to focus their attention on the screen before them, they let their mind clear of the day's thoughts and problems, and allow tension and tightness to leave their body. Brain waves slow down. Border guards step aside. Then voila, they're in hypnosis. Advertisers, who are highly acquainted with the workings of the mind, depend upon people to veg out in front of their TV so they can tell them what to eat, buy and think. Just like in our early childhood years, these messages go right into the subconscious without restriction.

What commercials are trying to sell to us is just one of the vulnerabilities we're exposed to when relaxing in front of a TV. Another involves the messages we get from the programs and movies we watch during this highly suggestible state. Shows with negative content can add to the emotional issues and negative beliefs of persons who are watching them, and even trigger an undesired emotional response. A person who suffers from anxiety for example, can experience a panic attack while watching a program with fear based messages. To retain greater control over one's emotions and comfort, it is highly advisable to stay rigid and alert when watching negative programming and only relax when viewing shows with positive content. Intriguingly, when one is not relaxed while watching TV, highly emotional or negative message content can provide a potential outlet for emotional expression.

Another time when people go into hypnosis is while driving a vehicle. Although more common with longer journeys, regardless of the travel distance, people will often enter some sort of trance state. The driver's focus narrows to the road and cars ahead of them, their mind empties of thoughts, their body relaxes, their brain waves slow down and suddenly their border guard is wide open. When this occurs, we shift into autopilot mode. We essentially zone out, while the subconscious drives the car. This can go on for quite awhile until someone cuts us off, or some unexpected stop or event occurs. Being in this state makes us susceptible to the messages coming off our radios and CD players, as well as the person or persons sitting in the backseat. While listening to self-help CDs and other positive messages can be good for us during this time, listening to negative radio programming or negative comments from fellow passengers is not.

Another instance when our subconscious is especially vulnerable is immediately prior to falling asleep and right when we wake up in the morning. It is that in-between time when we experience a feeling of grogginess and maybe disconnection. Although it may last only seconds or minutes, our border guard is fully open and our subconscious is once again suggestible to what we are thinking, feeling, saying and experiencing.

The very last thing you think of and say to yourself before sleep, and the very first thing you think of and say to yourself upon awakening will go right into your subconscious unrestricted. And being a goal driven sort, your subconscious will act upon it.

For example, if you say to yourself when you first awaken that it's going to be a bad day, like a self-fulfilling prophecy, you will most certainly have a bad day. If on the other hand, you say everything is going to be alright and that today will be easier than yesterday, you will be more likely to experience a good day. Regardless of whether or not you believe what you are thinking or saying, it is still highly beneficial to feed your subconscious positive messages and imagery before going to bed and upon awakening, so that it has something good to work with. Just modifying what you give your subconscious at these times can make a significant improvement in your life. It's also noteworthy to point out that the time prior to sleep is also beneficial for programming one's dreams to provide them with insights or answers to certain problems, as well as to initiate healing and releasing during sleep.

One of the most important concepts to remember when interacting with the subconscious is that what the mind perceives the body achieves. Thoughts can become things. What we think can become a reality in our experience. Therefore, it is best to focus on the positive, and think and speak as positively as you can.

Positive thinking and self-talk bring about the most positive experiences. Those who employ positive affirmations and imagery on a regular basis, both inside and outside of the hypnosis state, will find it easier to achieve their goals and dreams. Unfortunately, those individuals who received many negative messages and had many negative experiences in their life, will find it very difficult to think and speak positively. They can fake it for a while, but it will eventually be necessary for them to release the negative aspects of their past, so they can authentically project the type of life and future they want.

Dr. Masaru Emoto's fascinating book "The Hidden Messages in Water" demonstrates the importance of staying positive by exploring the vibration and dynamic of water and how a variety of sounds, words, symbols, thoughts and feelings can change its molecular and crystalline structure. Positive words, thoughts, feelings etc. were shown to have a very positive and beautifying effect on water while negative ones resulted in horrible distortion.

Because the human body is comprised of approximately 70 percent water, Dr. Emoto has drawn a cautionary link between a person's health and the state of water in their body. Presumably, if someone constantly focuses on the negative or is surrounded by negative people and situations, they would be less comfortable and healthy than someone in a more positive environment who tends to project a more positive outlook. The water factor provides us with another reason to get our beliefs, thoughts and feelings under control.

Aside from its vulnerability to thoughts, feelings and words, it's important to know that the subconscious cannot distinguish between what's real and imagined. Hypnosis takes full advantage of this knowledge to trick the subconscious into making the changes we desire. This inability to differentiate between imagination and reality can also be helpful in attaining future goals or dreams.

If one can perceive themselves being able to do something they've always wanted to do, the goal driven subconscious will view it as something that is completely achievable. It will then do everything in its power to help you realize that goal or dream. By giving the subconscious repetitive imagery and instructions regarding what you want, it will give you the edge that others with the same goal but lack of subconscious understanding will not have. Keep in mind though, if your goal is to compete at the Olympics, you still have to practice your sport in order to achieve that goal. You have to help your subconscious help you

There's one more scenario that I would like to discuss where the subconscious mind is accessible to us in our normal daily lives. Tired, bored, waiting for something or someone, or just not focused at the moment, what does one do to pass the time? They daydream. Staring off into space, zoning out if you will, letting your imagination transport you to another place or time, perhaps to another way of living, working or being. When this happens, you are actively engaging your subconscious. The thoughts and images you let run through your head can get stored in your subconscious without restriction. So, if you're going to daydream, whatever you do, keep it positive and while you're at it, go ahead and dream big.

CHAPTER 11

A GOOD HYPNOTHERAPIST

Hypnotist or hypnotherapist? This question causes a great deal of discussion and confusion. Let me illuminate you on my perspective. People with both of these labels can induce hypnosis. The difference between them lies with their objective for using hypnosis. People who use hypnosis for only entertainment purposes are hypnotists. Those who use hypnosis for more therapeutic reasons are more typically referred to as hypnotherapists, but can also be called hypnotists. Those who deal with more emotional and/or health related issues are also considered to be hypnotherapists.

A GOOD HYPNOTHERAPIST

Many people wonder why they need a hypnotherapist. While self-hypnosis is possible, it is extremely difficult to use for overcoming one's issues, primarily because most people are unable to maintain the objectivity vital to their success. Just like with meditation, people will often get sidetracked or have difficulty moving into an altered state without the help of someone else. Self-hypnosis is most effective when used for general relaxation and to reinforce positive beliefs and responses.

To really get the most out of what hypnosis can offer, one should seek out a hypnotherapist. A hypnotherapist will act as a facilitator in the process to help individuals maintain objectivity and focus, obtain more information and better deal with painful memories. This provides a much safer and efficient means for gaining greater understanding of negative experiences, releasing blockages and emotional baggage, and making the changes one desires. A hypnotherapist can also provide added inspiration, compassion, motivation and support to keep a person on track and help them achieve their goals. Together, the individual and the hypnotherapist make a powerful team for greater understanding and positive change.

Once they gain entrance into the subconscious, what's a hypnotherapist to do? They clean house. Like peeling layers of an onion, they walk through a client's psyche, find and discard all limiting aspects and garbage, create greater understanding, closure and peace regarding past experiences, then move shiny new beliefs, coping mechanisms and rules for living into the recently vacated space. Depending upon the self-esteem of the client, the type of baggage they're carrying and/or their level of resistance to change, the hypnotherapist might have to do some heavy negotiation or fighting to get it done. That's another reason why having a hypnotherapist is so beneficial. In the end, clients are given the new beginning they've hoped for and they can live happily ever after.

So, what should one look for in a hypnotherapist? What should one strive for if they desire to become a hypnotherapist?

Virtually anyone can be taught to get a person into a hypnotic trance and give them a bunch of suggestions. But what makes a good hypnotherapist cannot be learned from a book or a workshop. These less tangible traits are innate. You either have it or you don't. If you are inclined to seek out a hypnotherapist or become one, the following represents some of the qualities that I feel are necessary for a hypnotherapist to be most effective. This of course, is my personal opinion, so one can take it or leave it.

One of the most important qualities a hypnotherapist can have is sensitivity and compassion for others along with a true desire to help people. You have to have a big heart and an iron clad stomach to listen to the seemingly unending stream of problems and gut wrenching traumas that come through the door. Someone who doesn't care about people will not last long, that is for sure. Clients also need to know their pain will not be minimized or invalidated. Without sensitivity, a hypnotherapist can easily offend or hurt an already fragile person. And when that happens, the work has ended before it has even started and the client goes home unsatisfied and more miserable than when they first came in.

Another quality that goes hand in hand with compassion and sensitivity is integrity and the ability to create a safe space for the client. Trust is everything. Without it, a client will be highly resistant to exposing their innermost thoughts and feelings and thus be unable to be helped. Honesty and ethical behavior promote trust.

There is a code that transcends virtually every healing modality or therapeutic methodology "Do No Harm." A hypnotherapist must adhere to this principle without hesitation. There is no place for ego, manipulation or humiliation in this business. The client is not responsible for a hypnotherapist's hurts, disappointments, failures and trauma and should not be punished for something they had nothing to do with. People are usually quite vulnerable when they come to see a therapist. They need to know it's safe. A good hypnotherapist will earn their trust and make their client feel safe.

It's not enough to be sensitive and ethical, it's also important for the hypnotherapist to be as non-judgmental as possible. Personal beliefs and opinions must be set aside. Clients will often divulge experiences from the past about which they hold a great deal of guilt and shame. They are already judging themselves and do not need someone else to add to it. It is the responsibility of the hypnotherapist to help their client come to peace with their past and achieve forgiveness.

Judgmental comments hamper communication and expression, reduce a sense of safety and trust, and ultimately limit the results that can be achieved. It is important to recognize that no one is perfect, including the hypnotherapist. As human beings, we are all works in progress. Mistakes are inevitable and making them is not bad. They can be tremendous opportunities for learning and growth. When we learn from our mistakes and make better choices in the future, those mistakes can turn into blessings for which we can be grateful.

Another quality vital to a good hypnotherapist is flexibility. Because people are unique and will not all respond in the same way, it is important for the hypnotherapist to keep their bag of tricks and techniques broad and diverse. I am truly saddened by the one-size-fits-all approach employed by many hypnotherapists. I am even more saddened by the people who either view themselves as failures or regard hypnosis as something that doesn't work because of it.

A GOOD HYPNOTHERAPIST

Being a good listener and having good people skills is also essential to the job of a hypnotherapist. The ability to communicate not only affects how well one can impart confidence and comfort in a client, but can also impact the results that can be achieved during hypnosis.

Having good analytical skills and being able to ask the right questions is also critical to the effectiveness of the hypnotherapist. The most successful hypnosis practitioner will need to be a reporter of sorts, asking who, what, where, when and how, in order to solve the puzzle of their client's issues.

A good hypnotherapist should also be able to think and respond quickly. While there are measures that can be taken to achieve some level of control, the hypnosis state can be unpredictable. Thinking and acting fast can help make unexpected aspects from becoming a problem. Listening to one's gut intuition or instincts can also help head off issues before they arise.

A final consideration that I want to mention regarding the effectiveness of a hypnotherapist is the importance of them believing in what they are doing and in the potential for change. If a person has limited beliefs in the tool and/or the ability for a client to change, results will be limited or could even be non-existent. Unfortunately, as I've mentioned before, the same can be said of the client. If a client believes that it is impossible to change an aspect of themselves, and doesn't have even a speck of hope, then it is highly unlikely that they ever will.

In summary, I believe a good hypnotherapist is sensitive, compassionate, honest, safe, ethical, non-judgmental, flexible, adept at communication, analytical, quick on their feet, instinctual and believes in what they're doing.

CHAPTER 12

JUST ASK

The subconscious is brimming with information about us. Once you gain access to this treasure trove of data, do not hesitate to query it about anything that you like. When you want to know something, the logical thing to do is just ask. Quite frankly, it never occurred to me not to. Yet intriguingly, many practitioners of hypnosis fail to even interact with the subconscious, let alone ask questions that would help them be of more help to their clients, and more importantly, get the answers and resolution they seek. By establishing two-way communication with the subconscious and asking it the right questions, clients can be more successful and results can be more lasting.

When I want to know if we're going to be able to reverse a particular condition or just alleviate the symptoms to some degree, I ask.

When I want to know approximately how many sessions it's going to take for a client to achieve their goals, I ask.

When I want to know if the client will require the reinforcement of a self-hypnosis CD to meet their objectives, I ask.

When I want to know if it's necessary to go back or regress to some past event or events to resolve a particular issue, I ask.

When I want to know if there is nutritional component or any other physical factor as to why a person is experiencing a particular symptom, I ask.

When I want to find out if, when and how a client will be able to get off a medication or reduce their dosage, I ask. Note: Any changes in medication should be discussed with and coordinated with a doctor.

When I want to determine the cause of a client's resistance or difficulty in getting information or releasing something, I ask.

When I want to ensure that everything that was needed to be revealed and dealt with in a past event has been taken care of, I ask.

When I want to know if a client needs to come back for another session, I ask.

When I want to ensure that a client's work is truly finished and that we haven't missed anything and have released all contributing factors to the client's issues or symptoms, I ask.

The following is just one example of many scenarios where asking can be beneficial.

I've had several clients over the years who suffered from mysterious symptoms, discomfort or illness and were unable to get understanding or relief through traditional medicine. By simply asking the subconscious to reveal the underlying cause, the mystery was solved. Many of these clients discovered a more subconscious or emotional basis for their condition. Yet for others, it was just a matter of nutrition.

Each of these clients were consuming something in their diet or through supplementation that their body could not process in a normal healthy way. As such, the unacceptable nutrient caused an adverse reaction which led to discomfort and other undesired manifestations. By simply eliminating the identified nutrient or nutrients from their daily intake, their symptoms went away and their bodies returned to more healthy and comfortable states. On the flip side, those who were identified with having some deficiency also experienced a reversal of symptoms and discomfort by merely adding new foods to their diet or using supplements.

CHAPTER 13

HYPNOTIC TECHNIQUES & PERSPECTIVES

You now know what kind of junk we can accumulate in the subconscious and how it gets in there. You also know how hypnosis creates a dialogue with the subconscious so we can find undesired and limiting aspects and then change or remove them. And you know despite the fact that not everyone does it, we can ask pretty much anything of the subconscious and get some answer. But one final question remains. What techniques could and should be used to make the changes we desire?

There is no absolute in hypnosis, because as I've said before, everyone is unique. What works for one person may not work for someone else. Client responses can also vary by issue and even by session. Being flexible and having a broad set of tools and techniques at one's disposal will yield the best results. Unfortunately, many hypnosis practitioners restrict the way they use hypnosis and thus limit what can be achieved and even who can be helped by hypnosis.

Within the hypnosis community, there are many camps within camps regarding the whys and hows of hypnosis. I know I have my opinions on this subject. Of course, since this is my book and not someone else's, I'm going to share with you my own preferences. Please keep in mind, however, that the information I will be providing is not intended to be some all encompassing how-to guide. My objective is simply to expose you to some of the major perspectives and differences in the use of hypnosis.

I would first like to discuss the disadvantages and benefits of group versus individual hypnosis sessions. Aside from the fact that people typically have more difficulty relaxing in a group setting, the biggest difference between them is that one-on-one sessions allow for customization and personal attention, while group sessions do not. Rather than using an individualized approach, group sessions have to adhere to a one-size-fits-all structure and hope that it reflects the needs of most people in attendance. Group hypnosis also typically tries to accomplish change in just one session. The generic scope, short time frame and limited techniques utilized by group sessions, limit the results that can be achieved and rarely provide what people need to overcome their issue. Though highly unlikely, the potential for transformation after a single session can be a potent temptation to many desiring change.

Another important consideration when choosing between group hypnosis versus individual sessions is safety. Without personal attention, a person who has an unexpected negative reaction or experience may not get what they need to feel safe or to gain understanding, peace or resolution from their experience.

Despite what many in the hypnosis community will tell you, group hypnosis sessions are not the best vehicle for achieving permanent change. They are more suited for general relaxation and helping expose people to the hypnosis state during a workshop. Because it's more financially lucrative to provide a service to many people at the same time, and because people who have issues want to get over them as quickly and cheaply as possible, group sessions will continue to be offered and people will continue to show up to them. Unfortunately, many group hypnosis participants come away feeling as though they are not good subjects or that hypnosis doesn't work. The fortunate few who experience change from a group session will often find their results to be temporary. It is the rare exception that someone eliminates their issue in its entirety via a group hypnosis forum.

Now that I've potentially offended the majority of hypnotists and hypnotherapists out there, let's talk about another controversial topic, suggestion versus a more interactive and release based methodology.

Suggestive hypnosis attempts to override negative beliefs, behavior patterns and responses and create new ones, by bombarding the subconscious with positive suggestions and imagery. Suggestions can be either direct or indirect. Direct suggestions are more obvious in their meaning and tend to have a more authoritative or instructive feel. In contrast, indirect suggestions utilize metaphors and other less obvious ways of encouraging change. While some hypnotherapists prefer to use one type over the other, most will use a combination of the two.

Whether it's direct or indirect, the use of suggestion is one of the most popular techniques associated with hypnosis. It is so well publicized, many people think it's the only thing that happens when you get hypnotized. It feeds the common notion that hypnosis means to put a person into a state much like sleep and while they sit there silently with their eyes closed, a hypnotist drones on and on for some undetermined amount of time. And then with little or no memory regarding what took place, the client awakens a changed person.

Despite its perceived benefits, suggestion based hypnosis comes with a significant flaw. Because communication flows only one way, it does not provide answers or any means to get to the root cause of an issue and release the charge of negative experiences. This technique merely instructs a client to believe and/or do something that is in contrast to and presumably more positive than what they are currently doing and believing. It also relies heavily on the ability of the hypnotherapist to guess what the subconscious needs to hear in order to facilitate change.

While suggestions can remain with some people indefinitely, others may have only temporary effect. The key to any change with suggestion is repetition. Because the affect is cumulative, the more often positive suggestions are taken in, the more lasting the results. If one applies the rules of habit creation and listens to suggestions for a minimum of thirty consecutive days, they will also benefit from longer term results. Self-hypnosis CDs are commonly used as a delivery mechanism for suggestions, because they can provide a means of consistency beneficial to the creation of new habits, coping mechanisms and responses. The effectiveness of recordings will vary according to the suggestions used, as well as the commitment of the client to listen with regular frequency.

Most issues have some emotional basis and may or may not have complex trigger mechanisms. Suggestion alone is typically ineffective in these cases. Overcoming an emotionally based habit, behavior or response, or something with a complex trigger mechanism, normally requires a more interactive and release based technique like regression before a suggestion can have any chance of taking root. If the emotional component of an issue is not addressed, the person with the issue will generally revert back to the undesirable behavior when they encounter something stressful or emotionally challenging in the future. Without first getting to the root cause, suggestive hypnosis will most likely yield temporary results much like willpower.

I always conduct sessions with two-way interaction, and prefer to combine release based techniques with suggestions to get the best results. I utilize suggestions mainly for reinforcement purposes. Once the contributing factors of an issue are identified and released, suggestions are given to set the foundation for and program in new positive coping mechanisms, beliefs, behaviors and responses. Because repetition is key to how lasting or effective suggestions may be, regular exposure to them is important. I frequently create customized self-hypnosis CDs for my clients to use at home to support this purpose.

The process of using hypnosis to overcome an issue is like trying to make a new sidewalk. You have to first clear away the debris, so you can have a smooth surface on which to build the new path. Once the path is clear, a new framework can be established. Now the cement can be poured into the new frame. In time the cement will harden and cure and be ready to walk forward on. Getting to the source of an issue and releasing its associated triggers, blockages and negatively charged emotions is equivalent to clearing a path. Using suggestions to establish and reinforce new behaviors, attitudes, coping mechanisms etc, is like erecting the frame and pouring the cement. Having these new perspectives and responses take root is like waiting for the cement to harden and cure. In order to establish a habit of these new positive aspects, it will take a minimum of thirty days for the curing to complete.

CHAPTER 14

THE REGRESSION CONTROVERSY

Of the many hypnotic techniques that can be used to obtain understanding of our experiences and why we think, feel or behave as we do, none of them are more powerful than regression. This tool not only gives us answers, it also provides us with a vehicle for closure and peace. To regress someone means to go back in time to revisit one or more events from the past.

While regression is most often used to determine the major contributing factors and source of an issue, it may also be used to view blocked or incomplete memories or obtain information for curiosity purposes. Whether it is one's in-utero or birth experience, past lives or time between lives, or some traumatic or limiting event that a person either wants or needs to re-examine or uncover, regression provides a key to unlock the doors to our past.

The subconscious knows when and if there's a need to go back to the past in order to facilitate change, so it's best to ask. It is also best to let the subconscious lead you to what needs to be addressed, rather than presuming or forcing something that is unnecessary. This insures that no one's time is wasted and also prevents hypnotherapists and their clients from missing something vital to achieving their goals. If regression is necessary, one does not need to revisit every bad thing that ever happened to them. They only need to go back to those pivotal moments that either created or contributed significantly to the problem. In my experience, there are generally only three reasons why the subconscious would need to take us back in time.

The first and most common reason to regress to a past event is that the event in question is a key limiting factor but is unknown to a person's conscious reality. The missing link must be restored, so that the past trauma can be brought to a client's awareness and ultimately be neutralized and put to peace. A second reason for going back in time is to revisit an event that someone is already familiar with, so as to gain additional insights and information that will give them a means to put it behind them once and for all. The third and final reason for the subconscious to direct an individual back to some past experience is to demonstrate that despite a person's attempt to minimize or ignore its impact, an earlier event is indeed a problem and thus needs attention and resolution.

While most hypnotherapists who use regression prefer to get to their target right away, some prefer to do a gradual age regression before going to an event in question. The presumption is that when someone slowly moves back in time by certain age increments, they will be more comfortable with the idea of revisiting something critical from their past. I personally feel that age regression is unnecessary and should only be used if someone wants to re-experience key moments in their past related to a specific age.

Regardless of the approach or objectives one may have in revisiting the past, sadly, many hypnotherapists choose to stay clear of and often disparage the use of regression despite its power and effectiveness. Perhaps it's a lack of understanding on their part, or maybe it is fear. After all, it is a responsibility that cannot be taken lightly. Regression therapists are witnesses to the less pleasant moments in life. They also serve as reporters, protectors and fighters through the process. One must be prepared, strong and stable to walk through someone else's past and help them face the darkest moments of their life to find the light once again.

While those who choose to use regression are in complete agreement that revisiting the past is beneficial, there is a great deal of debate and disagreement regarding how it should be accomplished. I myself have very strong opinions about this very topic.

More often than not, a regression will begin with a request to the subconscious to take a client back in time either to a significant contributing factor or the source of their issue. On occasion, regression will be used to go to a specific time, place or experience that a person wants to gain additional information about, perhaps a business meeting or a crime scene, for example. Whether the subconscious is directed to a specific event or is asked to provide one that's relevant to a client's current problem, the biggest argument regarding regression is whether or not to detach the client from their experience.

Many years ago, when regression was just a baby, it revolutionized the hypnosis field. It opened new doors to gain greater understanding of ourselves as well as provide resolution to issues that were previously thought unresolvable. Given that it was a new concept, much had to be learned through experimentation. Understanding, rules and processes had to develop over time in an effort to improve the effectiveness of treatment. Two camps eventually emerged.

The largest of these camps believe that in order to effect change one needs to revisit their past traumas fully and completely, physically, emotionally and intellectually. To release the emotional charge of the event in question, proponents of this methodology require the client to re-experience their trauma in a full sensing way, over and over, until they no longer feel anything negative about it. It's kind of like moving an iron back and forth over a highly creased piece of material until all the wrinkles are gone. But unlike a garment, people feel pain. Having to relive that pain, whether it is emotional or physical, over and over again is nothing short of cruel and unnecessary punishment. At least to me it is.

Someone, for example, who has experienced physical beatings, sexual abuse, some horrific accident, or in the case of past lives, a violent death, will find it very difficult to move through those experiences with any degree of objectivity to come to any true resolution. The physical and emotional overwhelm they could experience during this process would not only be painful but could cause further trauma and damage. I am totally against this approach and thus belong to the much smaller camp that believes in detachment.

Detachment allows one to view information in an objective, safe and comfortable manner. Let me be perfectly clear, detachment is not the same as disassociation. Disassociation means to disconnect from one's thoughts, feelings, etc., disappearing to some faraway place outside of themselves. Unlike disassociation, with detachment, the client knows everything that's going on and is completely capable of connecting to the negative emotions and blockages associated with their past trauma without feeling physically or emotionally overwhelmed by them.

To facilitate detachment, a hypnotherapist will typically employ some imagery as they instruct their client to view their past objectively. A movie screen, doors along a hallway, a library book or a time traveling elevator, are just of few of the types of visual props that may be used to facilitate objective viewing of past information. Watching it, reading about it, or simply stepping into the scene as an observer or bystander, allows clients the amazing opportunity to revisit the past in great detail yet retain total comfort.

Despite efforts to help them maintain detachment, on occasion, a client may find themselves slipping back into the physical and/or emotional overwhelm of a past event. When that happens, it is essential for the hypnotherapist to reinforce safety, comfort and detachment, and have their client come above the scene so that they can once again focus on what they need for resolution.

If someone is presented with a limiting aspect from their past, how is the emotional charge of the event released in a detached way? One must first identify the feelings one has about their past experience and then discover where they are stored in the body. How? Just ask. Once the negative pieces are uncovered and their locations are known, they can finally be eliminated.

The removal of negative elements is facilitated through some form of imagery. Intangible emotions like sadness and fear, along with any associated blockages and discomforts can be given some tangible representation through imagination and then destroyed. This could be accomplished for example, by imagining the unresolved and limiting aspects being vacuumed or drained out of the body. The recently vacated garbage can then be disposed of by fire, acid or some other imaginary scenario to bring a sense of finality to the situation.

Clients often describe feeling a noticeable lightening effect after emotions are released, as though a brick has been lifted from one or more parts of their body, a brick that they were not aware of until it was no longer there. Thanks to hypnosis and the imagination, within a mere matter of seconds or minutes, a trauma can be neutralized and a client can feel comfortable, free and empowered once again.

Quick, safe, comfortable and effective, why would anyone choose to do it any other way?

It is important to note that if you take something out, you need to put something back in its place. Imagery and positive messages should be used to fill the void created when negative emotions, blockages and other limiting aspects are removed. For example, a hypnotherapist could have their client imagine the healing rays of a rainbow or the sun pouring into them, as they recite a list of good things such as confidence, patience and hope that should fill the void. Aside from moving new positive elements into the recently vacated space, it is also beneficial to instruct the subconscious to repair any damage done by previously held negativity. Where guilt, resentment or anger once reigned, there could be forgiveness and peace. Where fear once resided, there could be safety and trust. Where stress and overwhelm once ruled, there could be calm, relaxation and balance. And where pain once lived, there could be comfort.

Another point of contention amongst regression practitioners is what is deemed necessary for resolution. Some believe that simply becoming aware of the contributory event is enough to release its negative impact. Others, like myself, believe that a client must be brought to some level of understanding as well as emotional neutralization and closure regarding the past. If one is only presented with the reason for their issue and not given a way to come to peace with it, things could get worse. It's like opening up a can of worms and having no way to get the worms back into the can. If the emotional charge of the event is not released, a person's emotional response could become over-amplified and could re-traumatize them. The experience can be very similar to when a soldier who suffers from PTSD has flashbacks.

To illustrate how bad this can become, let me tell you about a client who came to me a few years back.

Approximately one year before they stepped through my door, they had undergone a regression from another hypnotherapist. In that session, the client's subconscious directed them back to a time when they were severely physically abused by a former romantic partner.

Understandably, the client had quite a bit of fear and anger and even rage regarding their poor treatment. The hypnotherapist did nothing to comfort the client, nor did they try to help them come to any understanding or peace regarding the situation. More importantly, they never gave their client any vehicle to release their anger and fear. In a nutshell, they basically told them, well there you go, that's why you're the way you are and now you don't have to be that way anymore. And without further discussion, the client was sent on their way.

To make a long story short, soon after their regression, the client began to exhibit greater anxiety, impatience and a shorter temper in their daily life. Thankfully, their uncontrolled or negative reactions never manifested while on the job. Their personal life, however, was another story. The fact that most of their relationships were imbalanced or stressful didn't help. But when the person they were dating suddenly became more negative and domineering, a surge of anger and even rage began to ooze out.

Unsurprisingly, it didn't take long before this client reached their limit and blew up like a volcano spewing molten lava. After enduring one nasty remark too many, they experienced an uncontrollable need to pummel their offending date. Thankfully, their suddenly ex-partner got off relatively unscathed due to their size and sheer strength and no charges were pressed. But the whole event and continuously rising anger scared the living daylights out of this client.

To address the problem, they chose to go to a traditional therapist who proceeded to call them crazy and in need of large doses of medication. Although part of them felt crazy, on some level they knew they weren't. They just didn't know what to do. And so they checked themselves into a special anger management program they heard about. Unfortunately, they felt even angrier when it was over than before they went in. Eventually this client realized that their issues became escalated after their hypnosis regression. Once they made that connection, they concluded that the only way to resolve their problem was to be hypnotized once again. Hesitant to go back to the person who might have contributed to them feeling crazy in the first place, they decided to seek out another hypnotherapist. That's where I came in.

I recognized immediately what had occurred. The regression caused the client to essentially relive the past. It reactivated all the associated feelings that they were unable to deal with before. To solve the problem, we went back to the upsetting events and released their emotional charge. We then used techniques that I elaborate on in my next chapter that allowed the client to confront their perpetrator and reassure and re-empower their old self, so that they would feel safer and have better relationships in the future. We also cleared a couple more events from their past that were blocking or discomforting them in their life, especially those pertaining to their relationships. As a result of our work together, this client was no longer angry and volatile, but quite calm, patient and happy, and better able to deal with life. Their current relationships improved, and their new ones reflected more of what my client wanted in their life.

In conclusion, problems can be avoided and results can be more effective if regressions are performed more thoroughly.

Another big discussion item that tends to put a dark mark on the concept of regression is the potential for false memory syndrome. Can one create memories in the subconscious that someone has never experienced? Yes. Can this be avoided? Yes. How? When communicating with the client while in hypnosis, it is important for the hypnotherapist to never, ever lead and always proceed like a reporter asking who, what, where, when, how and why. To avoid issues it is best to ask questions like: What are you seeing, feeling, thinking or experiencing? How did you feel about that? Then what happened?

Here's an example of the type of leading that can create false memories: You said that it's dark. Does that mean it's nighttime? Are you in bed? Is there a man with you? He's your father, isn't he? He scares you, doesn't he? Is he taking off his clothes? Is he touching you? Does it hurt?

A better scenario would go like this:

Hypnotherapist: What are you seeing, thinking, feeling or experiencing?

Client: It's dark.

Hypnotherapist: Do you know where you are?

Client: I'm in my bedroom.

Hypnotherapist: Is anyone in the room with you?

Client: No.

Hypnotherapist: What are you doing?

Client: I'm lying on my bed under the covers trying to fall asleep.

Hypnotherapist: What are you thinking or feeling?

Client: I'm not tired, but I need to go to sleep. I'm feeling scared.

Hypnotherapist: Why are you scared?

Client: I don't know.

Hypnotherapist: Your subconscious knows. It will tell you.

Client: I'm afraid he's going to come to my room.

Hypnotherapist: Who?

Client: My father?

Hypnotherapist: How old are you?

Client: I'm 12.

Hypnotherapist: Why are you scared of your father?

Client: Because he touches me and hurts me. I don't want him to do that, but I can't stop him.

Before I get too graphic, I think you get the picture. Good questions lead to accurate and helpful information. Bad questions and stupidity lead to trouble. A good hypnotherapist will avoid trouble as much as possible.

I think it's important to also note that while traditional therapists cannot create false memories per se, they can cause equally damaging aspects by pushing their theories on their patients. I've had a few clients over the years for example, who came to me in a state of panic and desperation, needing to know whether or not they were molested by their father or another close relative in their past. None of them had conscious recall of anything inappropriate occurring, but each one of them had gone to a therapist that repeatedly suggested that sexual abuse was the only explanation for their issues. After fixating on the possibility, each started to look at their loved one differently. This eventually led to behavior changes, as well as increased feelings of anxiety and depression.

During hypnosis, each person's subconscious indicated that no molestation had taken place. The source of symptoms that the therapist jumped to conclusions about came from less troubling circumstances. While there are cases where molestation is the cause of a person's issues, it is not the therapist's place to impose their opinions on others or force someone to make some inaccurate conclusion. Therapists of any kind should be very careful about what they say and how they say it, so as to avoid adding to a client's problems.

A final consideration regarding regression revisits the topic of group versus individual hypnosis sessions. There are a large number of hypnosis practitioners who regularly conduct group regressions to satisfy past life curiosity. I cannot impress upon you enough how very dangerous this is. As I've mentioned in an earlier chapter, group sessions do not allow for personal attention. When someone in a group setting goes back to a traumatic or confusing event from the past, there will be no one to help them deal with what they're experiencing or feeling. This can cause all kinds of uncertainty, chaos and pain in a person's life. My opinion is unwavering; this practice is unsafe and should never be done.

I think it's important to also mention that my concern for safety also applies to the use of pre-recorded hypnosis CDs to facilitate regression. Once again, a person could be presented with some emotionally disturbing piece of information and have no resource available to bring them comfort, objectivity, understanding or resolution regarding what they experienced. I know that the pull of curiosity can be strong. I would just like people to realize that there are better and safer ways to satisfy it. Hypnosis is not a game and should not be treated as such.

On a less controversial note, as I mentioned before, regression is not only beneficial for resolving an issue from the past, but is also helpful for obtaining more information to address a current concern or answer a specific question. A common example is to use regression to locate a missing item. A person can be regressed back to the very last time an object was in their possession. The potential for finding a lost treasure definitely makes it worthwhile to ask. Unfortunately, if the item in question has been taken or moved by someone else after that moment, there is no way of knowing what happened to it.

Another usage of a more directive regression is to revisit a crime scene. Whether you are a victim or falsely accused of a crime you didn't commit, regression allows an individual to obtain more details from the event that could perhaps help in getting a conviction or proving one's innocence. Please keep in mind though, that hypnotically obtained information isn't generally considered admissible evidence in a court of law. However, the information one obtains during hypnosis could lead a person to evidence that is permissible.

Another usage of regression is to revisit one's birth or time spent in utero. While clients may be directed back to the womb or their birth because of its relevance to a particular issue, some clients choose to re-experience these events out of pure curiosity. Regression allows a person a rare glimpse into these sometimes painful, but often times tender or even laugh-out-loud kind of moments. Clients are typically amazed by the level of awareness in their unborn or new born state, as well as the details that come through. It can be quite enlightening to listen in on conversations between one's parents or the chatter that may be directed toward their mother's belly. It can be both fascinating and alarming to experience that transition from the protective container of their mother's womb to the often too bright, too loud, too everything environment into which they emerge. But in the end, the love and welcoming smiles of those who await their entrance, tells them it's going to be alright.

CHAPTER 15

OTHER HYPNOTIC TECHNIQUES & PERSPECTIVES

As I've indicated before, to facilitate lasting change, one generally needs to address the contributing factors of an issue along with its associated blockages, negatively charged emotions and other undesired aspects. Aside from regression, there are a wide variety of techniques one can use to find and remove limiting factors from our being and facilitate closure or healing. The following is a sampling of some of the more interesting ones.

Early on in my practice, I recognized that there were some individuals who had exceptional self-awareness and knew exactly why they were the way they were or why they were experiencing what they were experiencing. Unfortunately, they still couldn't get past their issues. I wondered if there was a way to shortcut their release process and avoid revisiting what they already understood. So I decided to ask a client's subconscious to determine what was possible. I asked if we could just scan for the storage locations of negative emotions, blockages, etc. and release them without getting into the details of why they were there. After a resounding yes, their subconscious enabled us to find and unload tons of emotional baggage and barriers within a matter of minutes without having to wade through the minutiae of their associated contributory events.

There are many ways to facilitate the scan process. At the most basic level, a request is made to the subconscious to identify areas where negative aspects are stored so they can be released. The imagination is used to create some means for the subconscious to deliver its answer. A wonderful example of a visual framework that I often employ is an x-ray like panel with a generic body outline drawn upon it. The subconscious can use this x-ray structure to highlight or point to in some way specific body parts or regions of the body requiring attention. While this imagery promotes a more visual response, the subconscious will use whatever means or combination it prefers or deems necessary to communicate what it needs to. Instead of or in addition to seeing things, the client may feel, think, know or hear something that indicates where they have an issue.

Once their locations are known, the undesired elements can then be drained or lifted out via some magical hose, platform, magnet, etc. so that more positive aspects can take their place. For more technology oriented clients, negative debris can be represented by files on a computer. One can then search for harmful files, delete them, empty the recycle bin and then run a defrag to fill voids, promote healing and optimize everything with just a press of an imaginary button.

I have used this scan and release technique many times over the years when the subconscious does not require intellectualization of stored negative aspects. And while it is not always necessary, I often request a list of unresolved emotions or blockages that are located in the areas identified by the scan for both the client's and my own information.

Another way in which certain limiting aspects can be eliminated without having to determine their cause is to create some imaginary representation of the blockage a person is carrying. By giving it some sort of form like a fence or dirt on a window pane or stuff piled into a box, the client has the ability to look upon and quantify that which has been causing them difficulty. They can then make a choice to get rid of it. Whether they burn it, shred it, blow it up, ray gun it out of existence or use the "Force" like Luke Skywalker, it doesn't matter. Whatever method they choose, once the object is destroyed, the blockage it represents in their body, mind, spirit and life will be eliminated with it.

Sometimes the subconscious prefers to take a more high level approach to identifying the contributing factors to someone's issues. Rather than going through a detailed revisiting of one or more past events, the subconscious can provide a list of factors related to the area of concern. With the aid of a chalkboard, it can communicate in a bulleted format, the reasons, triggers or negative influences that are contributing to a client's problem. The hypnotherapist can then query the subconscious to determine the location of associated negative emotions and blockages in the body. Once identified, these aspects can be released via some form of imagery. Suggestions can then be given to initiate a permanent deactivation of triggers and encourage more positive responses in the future.

When someone has perpetrated something hurtful against another person, be it bullying, teasing, rejection, verbal attacks, physical beating, rape or heartbreak, sometimes there is a strong need for expression or understanding before resolution and closure can occur. Unfortunately, this may not be possible in the traditional sense because of physical distance or even death.

Thankfully, there is an amazing hypnosis technique one can use to fulfill this need.

Aside from facilitating communication with our own subconscious, the hypnotic state also provides a means to move beyond the limits of our conscious reality and connect on a more spiritual and energetic level. This ability can allow someone to communicate with another person regardless of their current location or state of being. This interaction is accomplished by connecting one subconscious to another. The process is equivalent to conducting a meeting in one's head. This meeting can only take place with those who are willing. We cannot force anyone to listen or speak to us even subconsciously. Thankfully, most people will be receptive to this type of communication and the closure it can provide.

To create a subconscious-to-subconscious link, one first needs to imagine themselves in the company of the person they want to speak with. They can then request that their subconscious's be connected to one another for the highest good. Once the link is established, the client can then confront their perpetrator, say things that they didn't have the opportunity or courage to say before, and obtain answers and understanding regarding why a person did what they did. This connection can also give the other person an opportunity to express remorse for their behavior and words. While none of this changes what happened, being able to express and get answers can be vital to someone's healing.

The subconscious-to-subconscious linkage can also be used to gain understanding of or resolve current conflicts with family members, friends, co-workers, bosses, customers, etc. The following are examples of situations where this might be helpful:

- A parent who has a child who has been behaving oddly as of late, but will not talk about what's bothering them.
- A divorced or soon-to-be-divorced person whose ex is inflexible about custody or visitation rights for a child.
- Someone who is having trouble getting through to a difficult employee or co-worker
- A person who is in legal dispute with a person or corporate entity
- An individual who has endured some betrayal or experienced a sudden unexplained breakup with someone they love

When people communicate in a more traditional and conscious way, all their wounds, fears and other emotional junk can get in the way of them being authentic or open to compromise or cooperation. Subconscious connections on the other hand, allow us to communicate on a higher level where most people want to get along, make amends and feel better. Because receptivity will be greater, negotiations and problem resolution will be more productive. Although the individuals with whom clients may connect will not typically be aware that any communication has taken place, they will still respond differently because of it. Clients who have used this linkage opportunity during their sessions are frequently awestruck by the amazing changes that result from their connection.

Aside from resolving conflicts, gaining greater insights and improving relationships, linking a subconscious to another subconscious can also facilitate remote healing. Remote healing means to do work on behalf of another person from a distance in order to effect positive change. Once a connection is made, the hypnotic subject can request permission from another person's subconscious as to whether or not they would be open to help in getting rid of some of their garbage. If consent is given, the client can act as a conduit to find and release negative emotions, blockages and other limiting aspects within the person they are communicating with.

Just as a client can receive answers from their own subconscious, they can also receive answers from someone else's. Just like they can scan their own bodies for blockages, unresolved feelings, etc., they can also scan another person's body for negative aspects. Using visualization techniques similar to what they use for their own release, a client can release the limiting baggage belonging to another. Countless clients over the years have reported back with stories of incredible transformations about the people for which they've conducted remote releasing. Pain relief, recovery from and even reversal of illness, improved behavior, greater emotional stability, conflict resolution and so much more can result from releases done via a subconscious-to-subconscious link.

It should also be noted that a hypnotic subject can also act as a surrogate for regression. This process can be complicated and the information exchanged can be exceedingly personal. And although possible, most people will not feel comfortable with this type of work.

Another type of releasing one can do involves buttons, triggers and negative influences that are actively causing undesired responses and discomforts within a person's life. To break the cycle once and for all, sometimes a more formal declaration and means of disconnection is in order. There are many imagination based scenarios one could use to reclaim their power and sever the ties that bind them.

An electrical switch box is a great example of a visual aid that may be used for deactivating these kinds of limiting aspects. But instead of circuitry, each switch represents a person, place, feeling or situation that could trigger some negative manifestation. This undesired response can be physical, emotional or behavioral. The subconscious can be directed to assign the appropriate number of switches for every button, trigger and negative influence that affects the client, and initially set them in the on position to demonstrate their current active status. The client can then choose to break that relationship by switching everything off and intending that the action permanently deactivates their influence over them. Once all switches have been turned off, the switch box can be locked up and hidden, and the key can be destroyed to prevent future reactivation.

In cases where a client's button or trigger is restricted to a particular person, the undesired linkage might be better represented by some sort of cord, ribbon or chain connecting the two of them. The client can then make a declaration to break the unhealthy relationship and then destroy the linkage and the remnants that facilitated the connection in whatever way feels comfortable for them.

Imagination based techniques are also extremely beneficial for breaking an addictive response. Imagery combined with detailed instructions can easily facilitate the purging of cravings, toxins and other undesired aspects from the body. Vacuums or special platforms designed to draw out these unwanted elements are just a couple of examples of visual props that can be used for this purpose. Once the negative factors have been drained from someone, the organs, tissues and other parts of the body potentially affected by years of exposure to addictive substances can be encouraged to heal. A person can also be instilled with greater discipline and control, as well as positive coping mechanisms, so as to make healthier choices in the future. Those who desire to stop smoking or refrain from alcohol, drugs or even junk food will find these techniques extremely valuable. Not only will the pull and desire be gone, but their bodies will reflect a healthier, stronger, more comfortable and energetic state of being.

Finally, in situations where a person has experienced something wounding in their past, it can be highly beneficial to have a client comfort and reassure a younger version of them self. What I'm talking about here is healing the inner child. There are countless people who appear in every way to be an adult, but in truth are children stuck at some point in their past. It is the traumatized or ill-equipped inner child who is making the decisions and running the show, rather than the adult. To bring the child to a place of peace and to allow the adult to take over, we need to communicate with the client's inner child and give them what they didn't get before.

To facilitate a dialogue, one only needs to imagine him or herself standing in front of an earlier version of their self. The client can then use what they've learned in their therapy to help create understanding in their younger self. They can also use this rare opportunity to hug their former self, reassure them of their safety, and tell them that whatever happened wasn't their fault. This kind of interaction can ultimately help their younger self let go of the past and move forward with a more positive expectation for things to get better. This will also enable the adult to finally resume control and begin to do all the things they need and want to do to insure their own happiness, comfort, success and security. Communicating with another aspect of one's self can be emotionally intense but extremely cathartic.

I've had numerous clients tell me over the years how powerful it was to speak to and comfort earlier versions of themselves. Many would feel a palpable shift as it occurred. Yet, despite my belief in being able to transcend time and space with hypnosis, I never imagined that I would have firsthand evidence to prove it.

After a client of mine was presented with an upsetting scene from their youth and was able to release the negative and limiting aspects related to that event, I had the client connect to their younger self. They were encouraged to do whatever they could to comfort that aspect of themselves and reassure them that despite things being very bad at the time, things would eventually get better and they would be alright. At some point during this interaction, my client's facial expression shifted to something like awe as they simultaneously said out loud, "Oh my God!"

When I asked the client what was going on they promised to explain later. Once they were out of trance, my client excitedly informed me that their interchange with their younger self was real, because they remembered it happening. Many years earlier, they had what they thought was an unusual dream. In it they spoke with a much older version of themselves, who told them all the things they just told their younger self during their hypnosis. They even remembered being intrigued by their older self's physical appearance. Although their earlier self was skeptical that things could be better, the client remembered feeling comforted by the mysterious encounter.

CHAPTER 16

IT'S A MIRACLE

Most of humanity has fallen victim to the notion that nothing short of a miracle can overcome genetic predisposition or the gloom and doom prognosis of doctors. The propaganda machine that works diligently to promote this limiting view offers up prescription drugs as our only potential for salvation. While drugs like penicillin, along with vaccinations and antidotes for horrific diseases and toxins are beneficial if not critical to our survival and good health, many allegedly good-for-you medications do not heal people, but rather trade one symptom for another. If you don't believe me, just watch a commercial about any one of the bazillion meds available on the market today. Notice how the list of side effects often outweighs the benefits and how some of those adverse potentials can be downright scary and life threatening.

The good news is that hypnosis provides a natural and safe way of accelerating recovery and healing, eliminating pain and reversing disease, if one has the courage to go within and face their deepest hurts and fears. There are of course exceptions to this. Hypnosis cannot re-grow limbs, at least not yet. And not all illnesses can be reversed. The extent of improvement or alleviation of symptoms that can be achieved will depend upon the stage of illness, the degree of damage sustained by the body, as well as any prior-to-life soul related agreements made regarding health. Only the subconscious can tell us what can and cannot be accomplished.

Cell biologists, quantum physicists and other pioneers of science have begun to prove what I've already witnessed in my hypnotherapy practice; if you change your environment, feelings, beliefs and thoughts, and come to peace with your past, you can overcome your DNA and free your body of illness and discomfort. Yes, Virginia, there is a Santa Claus. I'd like to share with you a few case histories that exemplify the often miraculous results that can be achieved with hypnosis.

According to the medical community, the disease known as Parkinson's is incurable. Three of my past clients would have to disagree with that statement. Although each one of them had full-blown tremors and a Parkinson's diagnosis when they first came in my door, each one is Parkinson's and tremor-free and living healthy, happy and productive lives. How is this possible? Through the power of each of their minds, they were able to uncover the source of their disease and ultimately reverse it. Can this happen for everyone? No. Is it worth a try? You bet!

You are probably wondering what kind of things had led these three people to manifest a disease like Parkinson's. Two of my clients diagnosed with this terrible condition had accepted a belief that they were destined for the same fate as their loved ones who had suffered from and died from the disease. And like a self-fulfilling prophecy, that's exactly what happened. Once they realized they had a choice and were not limited by their genetics or anything else, they were able to restore their bodies back to a healthier, more comfortable and tremor-free state.

The third client's illness stemmed from a highly traumatic early childhood incident of which they previously had no conscious recall. The unresolved negative emotions related to that trauma took up residence in a variety of locations in their body including their brain cells. The repressed memory and feelings laid in wait for decades before the subconscious began to manifest a variety of physical symptoms including the tremors of Parkinson's.

Once the trauma was brought to the forefront of my client's awareness, and the feelings and blockages created by the trauma were released and neutralized, the client's body began to heal itself and all remnants of the illness were gone.

This particular client never told anyone that they had undergone hypnosis or sought out anything outside their normal medical care. Because their experience was so personal and they didn't want to subject themselves to any questions, they decided not to mention anything at all. Understand, prior to their hypnosis, their disease was quite advanced and required them to see their doctor every three months. Their sudden and unexplainable transformation left my client's doctor scratching their head and having no choice but to conclude that something miraculous had taken place. As a result, they reduced the frequency of visits until there was no need for a checkup beyond an annual physical.

The next case I would like to talk about involves someone whose huge transformation was not only physical, but affected virtually every aspect of their life. My client came to me because they could not stop crying. Well, they could, but not for long. It was so bad that they had to take a leave of absence from their job. Prior to seeing me, they consulted with a traditional therapist who basically told them that they could not be helped. Thankfully, they saw my ad at their most desperate moment; otherwise, I shudder to think what would have become of this person.

The moment they stepped through the door, I knew that life had broken them. It was in their eyes, their voice, their posture, everything. With no true friends or support, no social life, tenuous family connections, a job they didn't like, a significant hearing impairment in both ears and a past that was so tragic it could be a made-for-TV movie, it was no wonder they were depressed.

This particular client also learned at an early age not to cry. If they did, they were brutally beaten. And so, they numbed themselves so as not to cry and subject themselves to further abuse. As life dealt them more and more tragedy and heartbreak, they tucked in as many tears as they could. On rare occasions when it overflowed, it created danger and limitation for my client and reinforced the need for them to be vigilant about suppressing their emotions. As years went by, no matter how sad or difficult their circumstance, they would not cry. But then, one day, something happened that upset them. Compared to earlier experiences, this upsetting occurrence wasn't nearly as bad. Yet it set my client on a crying spree that would last at least two weeks. All the hurts of the past that they so carefully tucked inside were now oozing out uncontrollably.

To make a long story short, when my client arrived to their last session, they were smiling and even giggling, but definitely not crying. Their body language and voice radiated pure confidence, relaxation and joy. They were also very expressive as they spoke of the wonderful progress and developments in their life.

This formerly disconnected and lonely individual became more involved in their community, joined clubs, made some nice new friends and even began dating. They were also able to return to work and feel more comfortable with the requirements of their existing job. This afforded them the time and security they needed to look for other employment opportunities that were more suited to what they wanted to do with their life. They felt strong, empowered and extremely positive about the future for the first time in their life. As if that wasn't enough, they got a bonus by having their hearing restored.

Because my client heard so many terrible things in their past, they decided to shut out the negativity by suppressing their own hearing. They did this unconsciously of course. Unfortunately, they also shut out all the good things in life too. Once they recognized that they could change things, we released the final blockages to their hearing and they were able to hear everything. And I suspect as the years passed, they were only sounds of joy.

While many surgeries happen in response to an emergency, others do not. The next case I want to talk about shows what can happen when we have time to prepare for surgery. The client in question required an operation to repair damage from an earlier medical experience. Unfortunately, it took many years for the technology to develop that would enable them to correct their long standing issue. My client was eager to get things fixed, but their difficult prior surgical experiences made them feel anxious about their upcoming procedure. Their objective with hypnosis was to make their surgical and recovery experience as easy and comfortable as possible.

We released the charge of all prior surgical traumas and began the work of reprogramming the client's previous negative perceptions of what a surgery and recovery experience is. All major aspects of their pre and post-op experience were dress rehearsed. Their body was primed to work in full cooperation with the entire procedure. All their vital signs were encouraged to stay at normal levels during their operation. Upon entering recovery, their body was programmed to expel the toxins and adverse effects of anesthesia, so they can think and communicate clearly and their stomach would remain calm and comfortable. Other preparations were made to accelerate their healing and ensure their total comfort, and provide for a quick and easy recovery. At home, my client listened to a customized CD recording to reinforce a positive experience.

On the day of the operation everything was in place. After a good night sleep, my client made their way to the hospital in a total state of calm and trust. As they moved through the check-in process and their pre-op prep, they remained calm and trusting. Their surgery went extremely well, and the time it took was dramatically less than expected. Their recovery was also more comfortable and easier than expected. They healed a lot quicker too.

And then at their six week check up, their doctor did a double-take. Although the surgeon knew they had performed the surgery, there was no evidence of the surgery in the area of incision. Because of my client's masterful visualization, the tissue came together so perfectly it looked like it was never cut. The doctor told my client that what they were seeing was not due to anything they had done, but something else entirely. When describing their experience, my client coined the phrase "Disney Surgery." And while there were no cartoon characters prancing about or catchy tunes being played in the background, a hypnotically prepared surgery can be easy and even joyful.

What is a miracle? Reversing an incurable disease? Finally discovering the source of a mysterious symptom or illness? Functioning in life without pain? Being healthy? Getting off medication and feeling good? Being able to protect the body against the adverse or toxic effects of medications, as well as certain treatments like chemo and radiation? Getting through a day without taking a drink, popping pills or shooting up? Feeling joy? Feeling safe and calm and being free of constant fear and worry? Sleeping through the night and feeling rested the next day? Feeling free of the past? Feeling positive about the future? Being able to function in normal daily life? Saving a marriage that once seemed unsalvageable? Realizing a goal that once felt unattainable? The answer to this question depends upon who you are.

I've seen so many cases over the years, where ordinary people experienced extraordinary transformation. Chronic aches and pains, incurable diseases, long term health conditions, mysterious symptoms, frequent illness, addiction, insomnia, debilitating emotional disorders like depression, anxiety, obsessive compulsive, post traumatic stress and phobias, along with a long list of other physical, emotional and behavioral complaints barely alleviated by traditional medicine and therapy, easily eliminated in just a few hypnosis sessions.

It may seem farfetched, but I assure you it is all very real. Humans are very powerful. We have the ability to heal our body, mind and spirit if we only take that courageous leap and go within. And when we do, we can create something magical.

CHAPTER 17

THAT'S KARMA FOR YOU

If you've ever felt a weird unexplainable connection, pull, familiarity, aversion or even obsession regarding a particular person or place, most likely you were experiencing a karmic response. Karmic what? For those who are willing to explore the realm of souls, lessons and past lives, there is a wealth of information available to explain even the most baffling of experiences. And while pursuing past lives can increase our awareness of the more hidden elements of life, it can also facilitate change and healing.

Much like the path to adulthood is lined with lessons from one's childhood and teen years, a soul's path and evolution is sprinkled with challenges and choices across multiple lifetimes to help us to learn and evolve spiritually. As part of our lessons, we choose the players that will help us along our journey. Whether it was the critical or fearful mother, the absent father, the cheating husband or the emotionally unavailable wife, we pick them all. As I mentioned before, people do not typically learn through joy, but rather suffering. Those who hurt or challenge us tend to help us the most. They are our greatest catalyst for change and healing.

Along with lessons, many of the gifts, talents, personality traits, beliefs and feelings we currently possess are carried over from other lifetimes. Tapping into past lives can give us insights into who we are and why we are drawn to certain places, people, things, time periods and situations. Past lives can also explain unusual responses or difficulties in our relationships and can be the source of a phobia, negative behavior pattern, chronic pain, nightmare or some other undesired and unexplainable manifestation. It's important to recognize that the garbage we accumulate in previous lifetimes can affect us just as much, if not more than our current life garbage. Keep in mind too, that the law of attraction not only works based on beliefs and perceptions we create in response to current life experiences, but from past lives as well.

Within the hypnosis arena, two types of clients emerge when it comes to past lives. The first type unintentionally discovers a past life when it is presented as a significant contributing factor to their current issue. The second type pursues them in order to fulfill some curiosity or to resolve some question. Whatever the objective, exploring one's past lives can be an amazing experience. I love doing past life hypnosis.

Obviously, the tool of choice to get us there is regression. Whether an event is from a person's current life or one of their past lives, the process is still the same. Although many of the issues we have in current times are similar to the ones we've had centuries ago, our past incarnations can oftentimes be more interesting. The rare glimpse of world history along with potentially exotic locales can definitely add to the experience. But to me, it's that great aha moment when a client finally remembers who they were that makes it all worthwhile.

Before I can go into further detail on this topic, I feel the need to go back up on my soapbox again. One of my pet peeves regarding past life regression is the tendency for many hypnotherapists to ask questions that make presumptions. For example, after directing a client back to a past life, one of the first questions that typically come out of a regression therapist's mouth is "what are you wearing on your feet?" The first problem with this question is that it assumes that the person is getting something visual. Everyone processes subconscious information differently and one should never get too comfortable with a delivery format given that the subconscious can change it at will. Secondarily, yet equally annoying, this type of question makes the presumption the person has feet. Another concern is that it focuses on a minor attribute of the person versus the scene they are being presented with. I prefer to ask what a client is seeing, feeling, thinking or experiencing and then go from there. If someone wants details about what the past version of their client looks like, they could ask things like: "Are you male or female?" "What do you look like?" "How old are you?" "What are you wearing?"

There are many types of information that one can obtain during past life exploration. The amount of detail that can come through will vary by individual, as well as past life memory. Names, dates and specific location information are the hardest to acquire, but not impossible. First names are a lot easier to get than last names. People will also tend to identify the continent, country or region of the world rather than a particular state, city or village. It is the story of their experience and the feelings they had where we find the most detail. Let's face it, most people don't really care where Sleeping Beauty grew up, they just want to know if the prince saved her and they lived happily ever after.

While many people typically enter a past life at a point in time that's relevant to their particular issue or question, one can choose the point of entry. For example, when the objective is simply exploration, many prefer to enter at the time of their birth and then sequence through various significant events along the way. When their death is not relevant to resolving their issue, one can still view their death if they choose. Whether or not there is an issue or question at stake, clients can also determine if any of the players in their past life have reunited with them in their current life.

Another popular thing for people to do is to get a summary of their past life. This may include the life purpose and lessons they went in with, along with what they accomplished, what they did right and what they could have done better. One can also borrow strengths from another lifetime and carry them forward into their current life to help them get through recent difficulties.

A common phenomenon that people seek out hypnosis for is to explain some form of déjà vu experience. To have déjà vu is to feel a certain familiarity with or to remember a place, person, thing, event, time period, etc for which you have no prior conscious knowledge. Knowing how to operate a piece of machinery you never laid eyes on before, knowing what's around the corner of a street you've never previously traveled on, understanding a language you've never studied or spoken, knowing what happened during some historical event that you've never read or heard anything about, or feeling an extreme emotional response to someone or something you've never encountered before, are some examples of déjà vu. A déjà vu experience can happen anytime and anywhere, and anything and anyone can trigger them.

While most déjà vu encounters are infrequent random moments in one's life, sometimes they can become a nuisance, and other times an overwhelming nightmare. Some people experience intense rushes of unexplainable thoughts, feelings, images, physical manifestations and even gut wrenching pain with frequent regularity. Many have described these unusual occurrences like a flashback or even a total zone-out that temporarily transports them back to another time and place. On occasion, a person will even black out for a period of time when something like this occurs. I've had many clients over the years who thought they were going insane, but before committing themselves to a psych ward they decided to see if what they were experiencing was related to past lives. Thankfully, by exploring their past lives, they were all able to put an end to their suffering and potential madness.

I've performed many past life regressions over the years. What follows are just a few examples of where past life experiences played a significant role in people's issues.

Just a year before coming to me, my client was assigned a new boss. Their initial response to the change was one of terror rather than the typical apprehension people have in the same situation. There was no reason to feel that way, but they did. My client tried to keep their fears at bay by telling themselves that everything was going to be okay and that they were being ridiculous. Unfortunately, my client's instincts were dead on. Their new manager was hell bent on destroying their career and reputation, yet there didn't seem to be any reason why. Open to the concept of past lives, my client was searching for answers to this terrible situation.

What we discovered was a long list of lifetimes with said manager. In the beginning, they were just two people in love. Unfortunately, their love became twisted. Insecurity, jealousy, fear then rage got the best of one of them and suddenly one of them was dead. This set into motion a horrific cycle spanning many centuries of alternating lifetimes where one kills the other. In my client's current life, their boss felt it was their time to carry out revenge or probably what they thought was justice. And while they weren't intent on murder this time, they were definitely trying to kill their underling professionally and emotionally. This had to stop.

After releasing many of the negative feelings that my client accumulated through these tumultuous lifetimes, I initiated what I call a karmic intervention and had my client's subconscious connect to their boss's. After much discussion and negotiation, they both agreed to sever their karmic ties and put an end to their feud. The war ended across time and space, and thankfully at my client's workplace.

The next case I would like to discuss is about a client who came to me with an unexplainable fear of abandonment. They clung to their parents with desperate fear from the moment they were born. Every friendship and every romantic partner was treated to the same choking neediness and desperation. Practically every day of my client's life was filled with constant and inexplicable fear that everyone they cared about would eventually leave them. Nothing in their childhood offered explanation or understanding.

As it turned out, the source of this client's issues stemmed from a past life in which their mother died while giving birth to them. Obviously, the mother didn't want to abandon her child, she simply died. But to this newborn baby it felt like total rejection. As if that wasn't enough, their father, grief stricken at the loss of his wife, emotionally disconnected from his child, causing my client to feel abandoned once again. I helped my client come to terms with what happened and then used imagery to unload all negative emotions and blockages they stored regarding their experience. Once their past life was neutralized, the client could move forward without fear and begin to enjoy their life and trust their relationships.

Years ago, I had a client who wanted to overcome their depression and relieve an inconsistent pain in their arm that had no explanation. Their depression stemmed from a loss they experienced during their childhood, while the source of their arm pain came from another lifetime where they were a soldier during the American Revolution. The arm in question was pierced with a bayonet during a critical battle. Thankfully, they were only wounded and ultimately lived many years past the war's end. Despite their survival, their experience during the war left a lasting negative impression that they carried into their current life.

This client's current life was filled with many challenges and you could say enemies. There were several people in their life journey who wanted to hurt them in some way. Encounters with a jealous boss or coworker that wanted to ruin their career, or a lover that broke their heart, or a selfish or difficult family member or friend that made life equally difficult, were all viewed subconsciously as battles similar to the ones my client fought during the revolution.

Each time my client was in the vicinity of an enemy of sorts, their pain would be reactivated. Their body was trying to tell them that they were in danger and needed to pick better situations and people to have in their life. We not only released the trauma from that lifetime along with its trigger for pain, we also released the self-sabotaging tendencies that led them to gravitate toward these undesirable circumstances, so as to avoid issues in the future. The end result was no more pain and a lot more positive, healthy and fulfilling relationships and experiences for my client.

Here's a case where a client's past life had a significant impact on their choice of marriage. The client in question began experiencing what they called flashes of knowing regarding their fiancé. These intermittent waves of thoughts and feelings were so strong and uncomfortable they made them want to call off their engagement. Despite a lack of evidence of any wrong-doing or undependable behavior on the part of their intended, this client felt a deep-in-their-core feeling that if something happened to them, they would not be able to trust this person to take care of any children they may have. Even though it didn't make sense to them at the time, they could not ignore the prodding of their gut, and so regardless of their love for this person, they did not go through with the wedding.

Years later, when they came to see me as a client, this big defining moment was finally explained. The person they were planning to marry years before was their husband in another lifetime. Tragically, this client had died in childbirth. Sadly, their husband refused their desperate pleas to take the baby before they died, and the child died too. Overwhelmed with grief and bitterness, their husband made an already bad situation worse by failing to take care of the children that were left behind and still alive. Despite the fact that my client didn't do anything wrong, their husband also blamed them for dying and directed so much anger at them upon their death that they stored guilt that would block and discomfort them in later lifetimes including their current one. But it was the anger and disappointment for abandoning their children that prevented my client from marrying this person in their present life.

The final example I want to talk about involves a type of karmic phenomenon that occurs before birth. Prior to each life, our souls sit down to create a contract for that life. In it we define our purpose or objectives for said life, the primary lessons to be learned, the key players that will be helping us in our journey, critical challenges and opportunities we will have, talents or gifts we will use, etc. I have often joked with friends and clients that we must have been given happy juice during this process to make it all seem so easy and fun. It's the only explanation I can think of for people to agree to the long list of challenges one has to endure on their path. Unfortunately, when the glued-on smile and dull haze wears off, we are left with the reality that life isn't always fun, easy or pretty, even if it ultimately helps us to spiritually evolve.

There is more than one occasion when a soul is given a glimpse of their contract while still in the womb. One of the earliest occurs during the first couple of months of their development. If someone is not comfortable with what they've agreed to, or something has changed, they can opt out so to speak. This usually results in a miscarriage.

Just prior to birth, the soul is given one last look at what they've signed up to accomplish before it's wiped from their conscious awareness. The knowledge can be frightening and even overwhelming. Some will want to rescind their agreement. A child may try to back up in the womb, as they are urged toward the birth canal. Many a tiny foot will press upon their mother's belly, trying to prevent the inevitable.

I've had several clients over the years who did not want to be born. They didn't like what they were setting out to do or what they would be experiencing along the way. Without happy juice, they were left with the often scary and stark reality that faced them ahead. Difficult births and even the most heartbreaking stillborn deliveries may be more about a soul having second thoughts and less about physical or environment factors. And for those who were born despite their objection, there could be unresolved elements from that moment that make a person less committed to living and more open to issues. And while hypnosis cannot turn back the clock, it can help a person feel more comfortable with going forward.

CHAPTER 18

ENERGY AFFECTS ENERGY

Have you ever stepped into an elevator or a crowded room or sat next to someone in a movie theatre and suddenly felt overwhelmed by a feeling that you didn't think you had? Sadness? Anger? Anxiety? Hopelessness? Did you ever enter a hospital or doctor's office only to experience some inexplicable pain that you didn't come in with? If the answer to any of the above questions is yes, you may be sensitive to the energies around you.

Kinesthetic, empathetic, sensitive to energies, huh? Hold yourself, this may come as a shock to you but everything and everyone on this planet is comprised of and emits energy. And just like there are good and bad thoughts and feelings, there is good and bad energy, or more accurately, positive and negative energy. Good or bad, energy affects energy.

Eastern philosophy and Eastern medicine in particular, acknowledge the existence of energy and more importantly, how it affects us. Their emphasis lies in trying to optimize the flow of chi or life force energy that runs through our bodies and everything around us. It is commonly believed that our bodies are surrounded by multi-layered energetic fields, and within the body are energy centers or chakras that relate to certain body parts and functions, as well as aspects of human experience and expression.

Energetic roads or meridians, as they are called, run throughout the body and connect to the energy centers, similar to the way highways have service plazas. And just as roads can become blocked or difficult, so can energy. These encumbrances can translate into feeling stuck or experiencing some undesired physical, emotional or behavioral response.

Both internal and external factors can contribute to energetic related blockages. Our thoughts and feelings, as well as the thoughts and feelings of others have an energetic aspect to them. This in part explains the law of attraction. Like attracts like, while dissimilar energy repels one another. And just like good thoughts and feelings make us feel good, they can create an energy that makes other people feel good too. On the other hand, negative thoughts and feelings that make us feel bad can create an energy that can make other people feel uncomfortable. If one is particularly sensitive to other people's energy, the discomfort they experience could be significant.

As I've mentioned in earlier chapters, we can store someone else's thoughts and feelings in our own bodies which unfortunately can manifest as a blockage or physical issue in our own life. It is important to recognize that this isn't merely a subconscious matter, but an energetic one as well. Other people's thoughts, feelings and energy can lodge into our field, rather than our subconscious, and still be potentially as destructive. Much like junk in our subconscious, this energetic debris can cause behavioral changes, inappropriate emotional response and even pain.

Along with people, places and things can carry some energetic aspect as well. For example, highly charged events like wars, accidents and murders can leave a residual energy where they took place. Objects can also carry an energetic imprint from those who have used them in the past. Going to a highly charged location or touching or holding a highly charged object in one's hands could cause some discomfort or undesired effect.

Shifts in the energy field of the planet can also create physical symptoms and mood changes. They can even trigger us to face unresolved issues and clear out garbage in our body and mind. Whether you subscribe to this or not, the earth has been undergoing a transformation for several years in order to raise its energetic vibration and bring about greater conscious awareness across the planet. Despite its positive intention, negative aspects unfortunately result from this shift. Earthquakes, tsunamis, temperature extremes, political revolutions, economic upheaval and downturns, as well as magnetic interference in our technology and communications are just a few of the less desirable manifestations of these changes.

While much of the ongoing earth changes have a more global impact, this shift can be felt in a very personal way. It could be difficult to distinguish between internally or externally driven disturbances in one's behavior, physical condition or emotional state. Adapting to these new energies can feel discomforting and overwhelming to say the least. Sometimes having a bad day is just a reflection of the reworking of the energies of the earth and the process of integrating these changes into our own bodies.

No matter what we do or where we go, we are all subject to the energies around us. Highly charged locations, like hospitals or funerals or crowded venues like concerts, make people more vulnerable to energetic overload. Rock/gem shows can be particularly challenging as the energy from the large volume of stones and crystals in the room combines with the energy of the attendees. Intense bombardments of energy can often lead to a piercing pain in the middle of one's forehead just above the brow line. This unpleasant phenomenon is commonly referred to as an ajna headache. The ajna, more typically called the third eye, has its roots in more spiritual or esoteric tradition and is believed to be the location where we receive and perceive information intuitively, outside our normal five senses.

Regardless of where or how one picks up energetic garbage, what can one do to defend themselves from energetic intruders? Shield, ground and cleanse. Just like doctors and dentists utilize shields to protect both their patients and themselves from the harmful emissions of an x-ray, we can use a shield of sorts to protect ourselves from the negative energy around us. Energetic shields are not physical, but rather a manifestation of our thoughts, imagination and intention. Despite their lack of tangibility, these energetic shields are highly effective.

One example of how to install an energetic shield is to imagine that a bubble of light, usually white in color is totally surrounding your body. Along with visualization, it is important to make some declaration or affirmation to intend that this shield protect you from all negativity of any kind all the time. It also helps to imagine that negativity cannot penetrate this imaginary shield, but rather bounces off of it upon contact. Making a daily regiment of visualizing and intending protection will help keep one comfortable and emotionally stable around negative energy. If you know you will be going someplace where there is a high probability of being exposed to negativity, it's a good idea to reaffirm your shield before your arrival. Using a command like the old Star Trek one of "shields up" is a fun and effective way to activate protection for one's self.

When someone goes into a hypnotic trance, their vibrational rate increases. A higher vibrational rate makes someone more susceptible to the energies around them. Knowing this, I make a practice of intending shielding during the induction process for every client, regardless of whether or not they buy into the concept of energy. This not only helps me ensure that my client doesn't pick up garbage while I'm trying to get rid of it, but it establishes a pattern of protection for when they're not in hypnosis but exposed to negativity in their daily life.

Certain gemstones and crystals can also be worn against the body around one's neck or in one's pocket to help ward off negativity. Black tourmaline, ocean jasper, garnet, snowflake obsidian, smoky quartz, amethyst, tiger eye, carnelian and howlite are just some of the stones one can use for protection.

Another protective measure we can take with respect to energy involves grounding. Grounding is another term for stabilizing one's self or making one's self more physically present on the earth. Spending time out in nature, touching something natural like a tree or grass, drinking or immersing one's self in water, consuming food or wearing or holding certain stones or crystals can have a grounding effect. Visualizing one's self standing barefoot on the ground and imagining that their feet are like the roots of a tree firmly planted in the earth can also result in stabilization or grounding. However it is achieved, when someone is grounded, they are less affected by negativity.

If all else fails, there's always cleansing. When someone picks up negativity from a person, place or item, they can release the negative aspects by performing some cleansing ritual. One of the best ways to get rid of negativity is to immerse one's self in water. A long bath or shower, or a leisurely swim in a lake or pool can do wonders to unload energetic junk.

Another powerful way of eliminating undesired energy debris is to visualize negativity draining out of one's feet while making an intention or affirmation to release the negativity. Certain gemstones and crystals can be placed on the body to also affect a positive shift in energy. Energy healing modalities such as Reiki, Esoteric Healing or Polarity Therapy can be used to clear negativity as well. And finally, hypnosis can also be used to facilitate shielding, grounding and energetic cleansing.

However you wish to handle the energies around you is your choice. But I would strongly recommend that you do not ignore them, for they will surely affect you one day.

CHAPTER 19

THE ENTITY FACTOR

There are strangers among us. Well, they may not be strangers, but there is definitely something among us. They are called by many names, ghosts, spooks, apparitions, discarnate, trapped souls, disembodied spirits, etc. I typically refer to them by the more generic term of entity. Most entities are portrayed as being something that one should fear. I feel it's important to shed light on this misunderstood phenomena.

An entity or ghost is someone who upon death, fails to make a full transition and essentially exists in a state of limbo. They continue on as they were at the time of their death, in an alternative dimension or plane that exists somewhere between the physical realm of the earth and the more spiritual realm of the other side.

A person may become a ghost for a variety of reasons. More often than not, it is due to some unresolved aspect from their life or death. Sudden or violent deaths can often cause someone to be stuck. Extreme guilt or responsibility for those they left behind could also prevent them from moving on. Faith is another big factor that could affect a person's transition. If someone doesn't believe in anything, their disbelief could prevent them from recognizing the path they need to take or the spiritual guidance available to help them move on. Those who do have faith, but prescribe to more fear based beliefs, could also be restricted based on those fears. And then there are those souls who knowingly choose to stay because of their extreme fascination with all that is earthly or physical.

Regardless of why they're there, the limbo like state of an entity doesn't typically provide the relief that a full transition would. Many ghosts continue to experience some of the physical discomforts and emotional overwhelm they had when they were alive. There is also a potential for some people to relive traumatic events over and over again while in that in-between state. This can make their days ahead very long and difficult. Therefore, it is in the best interest of every ghost to find a way to move on so that they can be at peace.

Unlike their horror movie or fictional depictions, most ghosts have no intention to do harm. More often than not, they are confused, rather than vengeful or malicious. That's not to say that having them around is altogether positive either. Sometimes our physical reality mixes with the in-between reality of ghosts and allows us to perceive and potentially affect one another. Although individuals with highly intuitive or psychic abilities have more ability to sense an entity's presence and speak with them, communication is generally not an easy task.

Despite an entity's reason for being a ghost, there is an aspect of their existence that makes them want to communicate with those who are still alive. Depending upon their strength and even determination, some ghosts are more adept at piercing the barrier and making the connection than others. Because of their energetic makeup, many entities will try to affect energy around them so as to get our attention. Flickering lights and static on the TV, phone or radio are common manifestations when an entity is present. Seeing something in the corner of one's eye, hearing an unexpected sound or voice, smelling an unanticipated scent like cigar smoke or perfume, feeling some resistance or chill in the air, or having something touch them that isn't visible, could also be an indication of a ghostly encounter.

Aside from an occasional electrical interference or weird physical sensation, an entity can unknowingly or knowingly trigger discomfort or other undesired aspects in the living. Remember what I said about energy affecting energy, well just like the energy of one person can lodge in the energy field of another and cause undesired physical and emotional symptoms, so can the energy of entities.

Some entities move about freely going from place to place, while others can attach themselves to a person, animal, place or inanimate object. When attached to a living being, they essentially remain in that person's energy field all the time. This close proximity tends to cause some disruption or negative effect if left unchecked. The extent of impact will greatly depend upon the emotional and physical condition of the ghost. Entities with high degrees of pain or emotional baggage like rage or depression will have a greater chance of triggering discomforts or inappropriate emotional responses within the person to whom they've attached themselves. There is also a potential for an entity to alter a person's behavior or create blockages in their personal and professional life.

Body aches, fatigue, migraines, impaired vision, nausea, dizziness, irritability, depression, anxiety, fear, anger and addictive responses are just some of the symptoms one can experience because of an entity attachment. Because all of these manifestations can be attributed to something else, it may be difficult to know if there's an entity issue. If their onset is sudden and unexplainable, and nothing seems to shift no matter what you do, it will be easier to consider entities as a possible cause.

What does all of this have to do with hypnosis? For one thing, some of the issues that clients come in with can be aggravated by or even caused by entities. Entities can also unfortunately interfere with hypnosis and the therapeutic process itself. They can prevent a client from obtaining information or skew the information they're getting, and even block the ability to do release work. Thankfully, hypnosis can also be used to detect and get rid of entities. The same thing that allows us to connect to another person's subconscious allows us to connect with entities. This link can be used to facilitate understanding of why an entity is still around and ultimately encourage it to move on.

Let me make one thing perfectly clear, if you would have asked me years ago if I could ever imagine myself interfacing with or confronting ghosts and helping them transition, I would have looked you in the eye and told you that you were crazy. It's not that I was frightened by the idea of a ghostly encounter. I just wasn't altogether comfortable with it, probably because like many other people I didn't really understand them at the time. But people and things change. So whether I liked it or not, I needed to get comfortable with the idea of dealing with entities quickly, because many of them would be brought into my experience because of the kind of work I do.

THE ENTITY FACTOR

Friends and former clients have given me the title of "entity release agent" and do not hesitate to contact me when they encounter an entity that needs releasing.

One of my first exposures to the entity factor occurred immediately after attending a hypnosis convention several years ago. A friend of mine called me out of the blue to tell me that we had a problem. I love the royal we. When I asked what our problem was, they went on to explain that an urgent situation had developed with one of their neighbors. Apparently, the neighbor in question was acting out of character as of late, and drinking a lot more heavily than usual.

I suggested that something may have happened at work to stress them out. My friend quickly dismissed my potential explanation, saying that it was nothing like that. After asking a bunch of questions and offering up a variety of other possibilities, I received the same response, "it's not that." Okay. At this point, I realized my friend already had an explanation in mind, so I just asked what that was. It's important to mention that this particular friend of mine is highly intuitive. They wavered from strongly suspecting to knowing that their neighbor had an entity attachment. This friend also went on to say that "we" needed to get rid of it. They weren't sure how, but ignoring the situation was not an option.

I laughed, as I recognized a synchronistic moment. "Funny you should say that," I said, "earlier today, I attended a class about remote de-possession." Incidentally, that class was with the late Irene Hickman, a notable pioneer in the world of hypnosis.

In this workshop, Irene discussed the variety of ways that ghosts can affect us and how hypnosis can be used to release these intrusive attachments and reverse the issues they've caused. Aside from an entity making their self known during a person's hypnosis session, one can use a hypnotic surrogate to connect with an entity that's attached to another person. Given that my friend was an exceptional hypnosis subject and was also highly motivated to resolve the issue with their neighbor, we decided that they would serve as the surrogate. Given that I had never done anything like this before, I was a bit apprehensive.

After bringing my friend into a nice deep state of hypnosis, we established a subconscious-to-subconscious link with their neighbor. Through this communication, we were able to confirm that there was an entity attachment. We then opened a dialogue with the entity with the same type of subconscious-to-subconscious link. This spiritual intruder made it clear to us that it had no intention of leaving, because it had exactly what it wanted. Let me be frank with you, this ghost was as belligerent and offensive as anyone can be. It took a lot to negotiate this situation to resolution. I'll try to explain what we learned as gently as I can, hoping this will not freak you out too much.

THE ENTITY FACTOR

It's important for you to understand that some ghosts stay ghosts because they can essentially continue to operate in an earthly or physical way despite a lack of physical form. By melding their own energy with a living person's energy field, they can experience much of what the person they're attached to is experiencing. For example, they can smoke, drink and have sex via someone else. Ewwwww, right?

Anyway, this particular entity loved to hang out in bars, loved the buzz of alcohol, loved to smoke and loved to have sex. My friend's neighbor provided a wonderful vehicle for this physically indulgent ghost. Of course, it also helped that the spouse of this neighbor looked like someone this particular ghost used to love. Discovering this little tidbit finally gave me what I needed to move this entity on.

When I asked them what happened to the person they loved, the ghost got upset. They didn't know. So I queried them about the last time they saw them. It was at night. They were driving home and something happened. They ended up hitting a tree. This was the same night this person became a ghost. To make an already long story short, their loved one passed away that same night and immediately transitioned to the other side. But our ghost, caught in a state of confusion, missed their transition point and went on to try and fill the void they felt but could not understand. FYI, this person had been dead since the 1940s.

I asked that their loved one come through to help this person go to the light and transition to the other side. The minute the entity saw the one they've always loved; there was no more resistance to moving on. They were so happy, as they went into the light together. It was a very touching moment.

Shortly after our work, my friend's neighbor was back to their normal self and their drinking was no longer a problem. This rather adventurous entry into the world of entities was just the beginning.

Just one year later, I attended another hypnosis convention. One of the many workshops I went to was with the late Carl Carpenter, who frequently liked to blend applied kinesiology (muscle testing) principles with anchoring techniques and hypnosis. He was also passionate about finding and removing entities. To shortcut their detection and releasing, Carl used a pendulum to facilitate communication.

A pendulum is a small weighted object attached to the end of a string or chain, through which the subconscious can transmit nerve responses that will cause the weight to move in some direction. The holder of the pendulum can ask questions and interpret answers based on the direction the pendulum swings.

Carl demonstrated his technique of using a pendulum for entity discovery and removal during his workshop and I have been using a variation of it ever since. Although one is restricted to yes, no and maybe type answers, the pendulum offers a quick, easy and efficient means to get the job done.

This method and any other method that facilitates communication with a ghost should not be taken lightly, nor should it be attempted without proper understanding and preparation. But with a little creativity and a very neutral attitude toward ghosts, there are ways to move along even the most complicated and difficult of attachments. I find the pendulum method most useful for clearing clients, myself, and my office before doing hypnosis work. It is also handy for removing ghosts from a historic site or building, someone's home, and even a hotel you may be staying at. Using a pendulum is also the quickest and easiest way to clear people or locations remotely. Just like with other subconscious type connections, time and distance become irrelevant.

Over the years, I've cleared hundreds, maybe thousands, of trapped spirits and attachments either while doing hypnosis or via my trusty pendulum. Thankfully, the shift that occurs is almost immediate. I would like to share with you a few more examples of entity releasing.

The following case illustrates perfectly how an entity can affect our therapeutic work. A couple of years back, I had a client come to me with a number of issues that they wanted to address. When we attempted to release some negative aspects identified by their subconscious in their first hypnosis session, our efforts were blocked for some reason. We hit a proverbial brick wall. No matter what we did, it would not budge. It wasn't even a question of their trance not being deep enough. The client was extremely relaxed and answers flowed freely in great detail. We just weren't able to get rid of junk.

I asked if my client was blocking their own release for some reason, at which point their subconscious responded with a definitive no. The only thing I could conclude was that something external was causing the problem. And so I questioned the subconscious to see if my suspicions were true. This time its answer was yes. It then revealed that an entity was interfering with the process.

I asked to speak to the entity and discovered that it was an old friend of my client's who had passed away several years before. This client was the godparent of the ghost's child. They had been haunting my client in hopes of pushing them to keep their promise to be there for their child in their absence. To the ghost's supreme frustration and disappointment, it had been years since my client made any contact with their godchild.

The ghost was worried about the trouble their child was having and angry at their friend for not doing what they said they would do. They felt their only option for getting my client's attention was to block things in their life as much as possible. And when my client sought to get relief from their own difficulties using hypnosis, the entity recognized this as an opportunity to be heard. They told us they would not let up unless their friend assured them they would fulfill their promise and check in on their child. Once my client agreed to do what was asked of them, we were able to release their garbage and bring about the change they desired.

Here's an example of a situation where my trusty pendulum came in handy at my office. One day while sitting at my desk, finishing up on some paperwork and waiting for a client, I began to smell smoke. It was the unmistakably stinky scent of cigars. I hate cigar smoke. Given that I was in a non-smoking building, I was both perplexed and angry at this sudden development.

I yanked my door open and marched into the hall to determine who was smoking. At the time, my office was part of a suite of offices. Surprisingly, all of the offices in my suite were currently empty, except for the one belonging to the receptionist. When I asked her about it, she said she didn't smell anything. Feeling both confused and determined, I had her come into my office to take a sniff, at which all she could do was shake her head and tell me once again that she could not detect any smoke or anything bad for that matter. I was baffled to say the least, because I was doing all I could not to choke.

I stood up on a chair and sniffed at the air conditioning vent to see if it was coming from the office below mine.

Even though I had nothing to base it on, I had no choice but to conclude that it must be the source of the mysterious smell. I went downstairs to investigate, but to my supreme disappointment there was no one in that office for me to confront. At this point, I decided I must be crazy and went back to my office. I practically gagged as I entered it once again. Despite not being able to see it, I felt like I was enveloped in a big stinky cloud. Once again I asked the receptionist to take a whiff. She shrugged and apologized for not being able to smell what I smelled, but thankfully she didn't call me crazy.

When my client eventually arrived, I felt compelled to apologize for the offensive smoke. They looked at me like I had grown horns or something and then told me if they did smell cigar smoke they would have to leave, because it makes them ill. I conducted their session with surprisingly very little coughing and sent them away happy and relaxed. I on the other hand was feeling something, but it wasn't anything close to happy or relaxed.

As I paced my office pondering this strange situation, I heard a knock at my door. It was my friend. I was so preoccupied with my dilemma; I forgot she was coming by to go to lunch. When I opened the door, she stepped inside and immediately began to cough. She then went on to complain about the cigar smoke and express her confusion given that this was a non-smoking building.

"You can smell that?" I asked excitedly.

"Of course I can. Who couldn't?" she said looking at me like I was crazy or something.

After I explained to her what had been going on, she found it very difficult to believe we were the only ones who could smell it. She also felt compelled to stand on a chair and inspect my vents and then ask about the office below mine. My friend wanted a rational explanation, but there wasn't one. Eventually the light bulb turned on in both of our heads and we realized that we were having an entity encounter. Neither one of us had ever had an olfactory (smell) related ghost experience before, so it wasn't something we would normally consider. Once I knew what I was dealing with, I took out my pendulum and encouraged Mr. Stinky to vacate the premises and go to the light. Thankfully, the minute he passed over, the smell was gone. Yay!

The following illustrates how effective remote entity releasing can be using a pendulum. Quite a few years back, I received a call from a friend of mine regarding a friend of a friend of a friend of theirs. This person had a baby who could not see, despite the fact that no physical reason could be determined. My friend immediately decided that this mysterious and rather tragic circumstance must be the result of an entity attachment and asked me to check on it.

Although I haven't mentioned this before, more that one entity can attach themselves to a single person. While I don't count them anymore, at this particular point in time, I had made it a habit to ask how many entities were attached to a person I was inquiring about. With my handy little pendulum, I discovered that this poor little baby had over a hundred entities in their field, especially in the area around their eyes. I connected to the strongest amongst the entities and asked them to leave this child and move into the light where they belong and bring all the other entities with them. Once they were released, to the delight of their parents and the astonishment of their doctors, the baby was able to see.

CHAPTER 20

OTHER SPIRITUAL PHENOMENON

Whether people come for spiritual reasons or not, spiritual things can happen under the realm of hypnosis. We've already talked about the effect of entities and the ability to connect to them during the hypnosis state. We've also explored how people can pop back into past lives to face the source of their issues or appease their curiosity. Aside from ghosts and past lives, there are other spiritual aspects that we can access during hypnosis. Just like with past lives, some occur spontaneously, while others happen because we request them to happen. Regardless of how they occur, these experiences can provide insight, wisdom, comfort and healing to the person who has them. They can even transform an individual's entire belief system.

As I've mentioned before, aside from lowering our brain waves, the hypnosis state raises our vibrational rate. In addition to making us more sensitive to the energies around us, it also allows us to communicate with other planes or dimensions of existence. This same ability which lets us communicate with entities in the in-between, can also let us communicate with departed loved ones, guides, guardian angels and other spiritual entities from what many people call the other side.

The loss of someone can be one of the most difficult and defining moments one can experience. Grief can twist and morph and become out of control to the point that it becomes a blockage in a person's life. It can eat away to such a degree that it can prevent someone from doing more than just existing, let alone experiencing any true joy in their life. Fear of death and/or a limited belief system can also cause a great deal of disruption and pain with the passing of a loved one.

One of the more comforting of spiritual phenomena during hypnosis is the ability to connect or visit with departed loved ones. It can facilitate closure especially in the case when someone we loved died suddenly and there was no opportunity to say good bye or I love you. This is also extremely helpful for obtaining some degree of understanding and resolution in the case of suicide or murder. Regardless of the reason for passing, this special communication vehicle also allows us to feel the continuing connection and love that exists beyond time and space and the physical reality of the earth. This reassuring aspect can be vital in helping someone overcome their grief. Experiencing the comforting messages and love of someone who has passed can also alleviate the fears one has regarding death and even expand the limited belief set of the client. Above all, the ability to connect with departed loved ones during hypnosis allows the people who have loved us to reach out from afar and give us one final gift of peace.

For those who believe in spiritual helpers like guides and guardian angels, the hypnosis state offers a rare opportunity to connect to them. Just like with other spiritual experiences, they can occur unrequested or be initiated by the client. These special meetings can provide us with insights into our own existence, our soul path, as well as more universal concepts. They can also give us support, encouragement and strength during difficult times in our life.

Another area that is popular within the hypnosis arena is the ability to connect to pets, both living and deceased. Dogs and cats not only have a level of consciousness but a soul cycle similar to humans, only much less complicated. I know this may sound like fantasy or wishful thinking, but it's not. Pets also have life purposes and reincarnate much like the people in their lives. Through hypnosis, we can communicate with our dogs and cats to better understand changes in their behavior, determine if they are experiencing any discomfort, or reassure them when they're confused or upset. This alternative state of consciousness can also allow us to access their wishes regarding the question of continuation of their life, and even connect with them when they've passed on.

And while my next discussion item doesn't fall entirely under the realm of spiritual phenomenon, it can have spiritual implications as well as applications. The concept of out-of- body travel or remote viewing fascinates us and ignites our imagination. It is also frequently lumped together with hypnosis, but what it really is and how it can be initiated is not widely known.

Out-of-body travel or remote viewing requires a type of disconnection from the physical body. This temporary separation allows the more energetic and spiritual part of us to move beyond the normal limits of time, space, distance and dimensional existence. It makes it possible for one to leave their current location and time and visit any person, place or era they choose. Why would someone do this? Perhaps the most common reason is pure curiosity. On the other hand, many choose to engage in something like this to satisfy more serious or even sinister motives. It is common knowledge that governments throughout the world have experimented with this very state to see how it can aid their military objectives, amongst other things.

OTHER SPIRITUAL PHENOMENON

With knowledge comes power. Its allure can be quite potent. Unfortunately, people can get more than they bargained for.

Out-of-body travel or remote viewing is most typically activated during sleep, meditation or while in hypnosis with or without a person's intention. In rare instances, it can occur spontaneously while a person is still conscious.

Information gathering during hypnosis does not require any disconnection from the body and generally relies on subconscious-to-subconscious linkage for answers outside an individual. This kind of connection is generally safe, especially when protection is intended. On the other hand, going out of one's body can be quite a risky proposition. The protective aspects one evokes during hypnosis are not carried with the person's spirit and energy when they leave. Disconnection makes one susceptible to the positive or negative energy and intentions of other people or entities they encounter in their travels. As a result, remote viewers can pick up undesired garbage or attachments quite easily. One can also take on physical issues as well. The following case helps illustrate our vulnerability during out-of-body travel.

Several years ago, I had a client who hadn't heard from her son in a few days and was feeling extremely curious about how he was doing. Once she was in hypnosis, rather than connecting to his subconscious, she decided to pop out of her body to check things out. I tried to discourage her, but she wouldn't have any of it. Next thing I know, she's standing in her son's room where she found him sick as a dog. She went to put her arms around him and see if she could test his forehead for a fever. Before she could say another word, she was coughing her brains out and gasping for air.

Apparently, the simple act of touching his energy field with her own caused her to take on her son's illness and the symptoms that came with it. I demanded that she return to her body and then proceeded to clean up the mess she brought back with her. It took me a good half an hour before she could breathe okay and not cough anymore. It was clear that all the protective intentions we made for her during her session were thrown out the window when she left her body. Unsurprisingly, she didn't do that again. Lesson learned. By the way, when my client spoke to her son later that evening, he confirmed that he was sick and was waiting desperately for the antibiotics he just picked up that day to take affect.

While information obtained through out-of-body travel can be intriguing and even helpful, its risk is not something to take lightly. Shortly after my client's out-of-body fiasco, I read a book that detailed a man's experience in one of our own government's remote viewing programs. Unfortunately, its title escapes me. The horrifying truth about this experiment was that most of its participants were left broken physically, emotionally, mentally and spiritually by their involvement. Thankfully, through his work with a Native American shaman, the book's author was eventually able to repair some of the damage to his life and lived to tell the story. It's a cautionary tale for those who may be inclined to dabble with something like this.

CHAPTER 21

IT'S A PROCESS

Many people are under the impression that one hypnosis session will magically wipe away all of their problems, undesired behaviors and manifestations. In truth, it is the exception rather than the rule for someone to complete their work in a single session, let alone have instant and complete change. So how long does it really take and what can people expect in terms of results? The answer is that it depends.

Numerous hypnotherapists require clients to attend a certain number of sessions regardless of the type of issue they are working on or the extent of factors that may be contributing to the problem. Other hypnotherapists may arbitrarily assign a particular number of sessions to each type of issue they work with. Clients will then be required to attend that specified number of sessions regardless of the complexity of their issue. Hypnotherapists may also choose to have clients attend sessions until their issues appear to be gone. Some will even treat their hypnosis work like a traditional therapist would, and have clients come on and off over a designated period of time that could extend for years. Very few do what I do.

I prefer to let a client's subconscious lead us to all that we need to resolve their issues and tell us when we're done. At the end of every hypnosis session, I ask the subconscious if we've gotten everything that's been contributing to the problem. If the subconscious indicates there's more junk to release, the client comes back for another session. When it communicates that all negative, limiting and discomforting aspects are gone and that there's nothing more that needs to be done for resolution, my client's work is complete. When the subconscious determines the number of sessions, clients only pay for what they need. But more importantly, they don't have to worry about missing something vital to their healing or having their issue return in the future.

The subconscious is very efficient and can get us through large amounts of junk very quickly. The number of hypnosis sessions required will depend upon a client's goals, how easy they relax and how deep-seated the issue is.

While some clients can take more or less time, most achieve resolution within 3 to 5 sessions. For children and teens, the average typically falls between 1 and 3 sessions.

When a client has completed the number of sessions deemed necessary by their subconscious, will all undesired manifestations be completely gone when they reach the end of their last session? Maybe. Results will vary by individual. And because of a variety of factors controlled by the subconscious, there could be some delay as to when and how a person's work takes effect. Unfortunately, it could require a good deal of patience before a client reaps the benefits of their hard work.

Some clients may notice a big difference right away. Others may see little or no change until their last session is complete, and then as if a switch has been flipped, they feel totally different. The more typical experience is a gradual reduction in symptoms or undesired behaviors as a client goes through each session. In these cases, changes are not usually sustainable until all work is complete. It is important to stay positive and hopeful and focus on the glimpses of shifting and improvement rather than any temporary setbacks. Eventually, one's patience will be rewarded and results will be fully realized and maintainable. It is important to note however, that there could be an additional 30 days of waiting before results can be seen if a person requires the reinforcement of a self-hypnosis CD to meet their goals.

IT'S A PROCESS

As to when an individual may experience total transformation, it will depend upon the issues at stake along with the subconscious' knowledge and desire regarding what's best for the client. It's important to recognize that the physical is typically the last level to manifest change. Many things have to be adjusted behind the scenes before the body can begin to transform itself. The time it takes for healing and change to be complete will vary by individual, as well as the physical issue being addressed.

In rare instances, the subconscious will postpone when results appear or finalize. I've discussed some of the potential reasons why the subconscious may hold things up in Chapter 6. Aside from those previously mentioned circumstances, delays can also occur because of a client's inability to deal with certain information or perspectives at a particular point in time. In an effort to do what's best for the client, the subconscious may limit what it reveals at a given moment and then wait until some future date it deems more appropriate to bring a new layer or piece of the puzzle to the surface. Once all layers are finally known and dealt with, results should take full effect.

Until all the work is done and all the desired changes have taken full and lasting residence within the subconscious, a client may manifest a variety of symptoms in response to their experience. This is often referred to as processing. While waiting for the dust to settle so to speak, one can have increased dream activity, flashes of memories, emotional sensitivity and physical discomfort, not to mention some releases of the physical kind. Those in transition can also find themselves less talkative or more expressive than usual.

Another aspect of processing is that as junk gets staged by the subconscious for release, our issues can sometimes be aggravated prior to their leaving. As undesired elements get moved from the deeper recesses of the warehouse and are placed onto the loading dock and made ready for shipping, their closer proximity allows them to poke us more easily. This means, things can get worse before they get better.

Thankfully, processing is temporary, but its presence can be almost as unsettling as the information clients may uncover in their sessions. While many revisit much of what they already know, the subconscious may bring to the forefront of awareness, hidden elements that can offer explanation of our greatest mysteries and change everything we thought we knew. These aha moments can shake the very foundation upon which people have based their lives. Sometimes processing is just about coming to a level of acceptance with these very new and sometimes startling perspectives.

I often think our work-in-process is like cleaning out a closet. We have to thoroughly examine its contents and decide what to keep and what to discard. The junk we acquire over the years is like clothing that no longer fits or is so completely out of style we would be laughed at if we wore it outside of a Halloween bash. We also have to consider the amount of space we have. If we want room for something new, we have to let go of something old.

Many times in cleaning out our closets, piles of clothing, accessories and hangers are strewed out on the floor in temporary heaps before decisions can be finalized and our organizational strategy can be implemented. This transitional state leaves our stuff vulnerable to those who may pass by, as well as our own devices. Crushed or torn garments, bent belt buckles, nicked shoe leather, and heaven forbid one of the already few and far between clip hangers broken in some random occurrence before they could be safely returned to our closet. The whole experience could be quite disconcerting. But once our work is done, all we can do is beam with pride and satisfaction at the clean, organized and beautiful results of our effort and think it was all worth it. Because it is.

CONCLUSION

Despite what society says, we are not doomed by prognosis or genetics. People have choice and power. Moreover, it is not bad or selfish to focus on one's self and feel better. There are numerous tools available to those who desire change. One of the most powerful and effective means for transformation and healing is hypnosis. What can be achieved is only limited by one's willingness to believe, along with one's courage and hope to face their darkest moments, seek out lost truths and reclaim their power. Be brave, positive and hopeful, my dear readers. Choose to clean out the cobwebs in your mind and invite peace, happiness and good health into your life. Think big. Believe only good things. Expect only the best. And know that you are worth it.

CONCLUSION

As for my fellow hypnotherapists, I know I have challenged many of the long held ways of the hypnosis world. While I don't pretend to know everything about the mind or hypnosis, I felt it was important to share my own experiences and perspective. Although there are many hypnotherapists out there making a difference, I believe there are some hypnosis practitioners who should rethink their choice of profession. I also believe that many more hypnotherapists in the field can do so much more then they are already doing. And as for the few and proud who challenge the status quo like myself, I honor and applaud you for your courage to be different and encourage you to keep doing what you're already doing.

And as for the medical community, I will continue to hope that one day soon you will truly accept that human beings are more than their bodies. To ignore or minimize the influence of thoughts, feelings, energy and spirit on one's health and wellbeing is to limit one's healing potential. It is time to embrace the multifaceted nature of human beings and expand your partnership with alternative healing practitioners. I challenge you to break free from the pressures of the pharmaceutical companies who seek to limit our choices. I ask you to revise current insurance practices and policy to include all means of healing in their coverage and make alternatives like hypnosis accessible to everyone. By transforming healthcare to a more holistic emphasis, miracles can become as commonplace as technology is in our society today. And when that happens, we will all have cause for celebration.

ABOUT THE AUTHOR

For more than 16 years as a certified hypnotherapist, Dawn Wheeler has harnessed and honed the tool of hypnosis to help people transform virtually every aspect of their lives. Her own uniquely comprehensive approach, integrating body, mind, spirit and energy concepts, enables clients to achieve lasting and effective change. These changes are experienced physically, emotionally, mentally, behaviorally and spiritually. Dawn is a certified member of the International Medical and Dental Hypnotherapy Association (IMDHA). She currently resides in Michigan with her husband.

Made in the USA
Middletown, DE
13 June 2019